TOM NEHA

APPLES
for the
MIND

CREATING **EMOTIONAL BALANCE,**
PEAK PERFORMANCE & LIFELONG WELLBEING

FORMIDABLE
PRESS

Don't forget to claim the templates and downloads that go with this book!

To help you put many of the ideas in this book into practice quickly, I have created some easy-to-use bonuses. They are free to download and use.

Grab them at:

tomnehmy.com/applesupgrades

Copyright © 2019 Tom Nehmy, PhD

All rights reserved.

No part of this book may not be reproduced, stored in a retrieval system, or transmitted, in any form or by any means, electronic, mechanical, photocopying, recording, or otherwise, in whole or in part, without written permission from the publisher, except in the case of brief quotations embodied in critical reviews and certain other non-commercial uses permitted by copyright law. For permission requests, contact the publisher via the website below.

Formidable Press

www.formidablepress.com

ISBN: 978-0-6485004-0-7 Paperback
ISBN: 978-0-6485004-2-1 Hardcover

Legal Notice
The Purchaser or Reader of this publication assumes responsibility for the use of these materials and information. The Author and Publisher assume no responsibility or liability whatsoever on the behalf of any Purchaser or Reader of these materials and information.

The names, details, and circumstances of those mentioned in this publication have been changed to protect their privacy. Examples have frequently been aggregated and anonymised. This publication is not intended as a substitute for the advice of health care professionals.

This book has been prepared in Australian English.

Cover and interior design by Damonza.com

To Jasper

May an abundance of fruit always grow on your tree.

CONTENTS

CHAPTER 1

WELLBEING IS MORE IMPORTANT THAN HAPPINESS

As DAVID SAT across from me, he looked spent.

Despite having a successful business, money in the bank, a loving wife and two gorgeous kids, his life had become a blur of irritability and stress. Even when he had quality time with family and friends, he felt the pleasure had gone. His wife complained that he was no longer the man she married, and David agreed.

How is it that David came to be sitting on my therapist's couch?

It had nothing to do with a traumatic childhood or an imbalance in his brain chemistry. He had simply followed the life plan so many of us assume we should: if we work hard, be a good person, have a family, earn money, happiness will follow. But the happiness that David assumed would follow eluded him. He felt deflated, defeated, and ripped off. If he had done everything right, why didn't he feel good? He met society's definition of success but still something was missing. Didn't he deserve to be happy? The mistake David made was to confuse happiness—feeling good—with *wellbeing*.

Pursuing good feelings alone does not equate to fulfilment. Meeting society's expectations for a successful life does not always feel good. Pursuing happy feelings is not the same thing as cultivating wellbeing, which is the heart of our deep enjoyment of life.

Throughout my career as a clinical psychologist, I've made these and other crucial observations. The essential lessons I present to you here are the result of my discoveries over fifteen years, working with literally thousands of clients: in my private practice, my workshops, and subsequently my wellbeing program, *Healthy Minds* (www.healthymindsprogram.com).

Time and again, I saw people, like David, who had been sold the same happiness myth and were bewildered to find their spark for life had dimmed. Others were existing within a meek middle-ground where they were not experiencing a psychological problem *per se* but also were not fulfilling their potential and operating at peak performance. The strategic focus on wellbeing that I developed to help my clients, then expanded into the Healthy Minds program, has worked for thousands of people who felt stuck, let down, or frustrated with life. Not only did it help them overcome problems, it was also a doorway to greater functioning.

I was able to help David recover. He went from being stuck to having a life that was more satisfying and healthy than before. His focus quickly shifted from struggling to achieving new goals.

The methods I used to help David and many other clients who came to me with symptoms of anxiety, depression, and chronic stress, focus on a specific set of skills and concepts that don't merely return people to their prior good-enough functioning, but helps them to reach new levels of wellbeing and effectiveness in all aspects of life.

I noticed that even when people were functioning *fairly* well, these concepts could be applied in a proactive way to create even higher levels of mental health and peak performance. Because being *very* well is associated with higher motivation, engagement, energy levels, clear thinking, and creativity.

By switching his focus from attaining positive mood states to his overall wellbeing, David was able to recover his good feelings while also creating enduring mental health, higher performance at work, and resilience in the face of life's inevitable challenges.

Of all the crucial components to wellbeing that I taught, each of which I will explain in the pages that follow, the one most commonly lacking was a clear understanding of *psychological skills*. While people readily understood the importance of factors like diet and exercise in being generally healthy, the concepts underlying a balanced and healthy emotional life were simply not common knowledge. Concepts that I took for granted like realistic, helpful thinking; how to manage emotional impulses; building flexibility; understanding stress; and self-compassion, were not well known to my clients at the beginning of therapy. Unlike daily physical health routines, these important daily *mental health* skills and habits tended to be unfamiliar and poorly understood.

As I noticed more and more clients grow into effective self-managers of their wellbeing, I became preoccupied with a captivating question: what if we could target these key psychological factors in advance of the life events that might drive someone to therapy? What if the clients in front of me had been taught the skills and knowledge I was about to teach them *before* their problem arose? And if we did teach these skills in advance, would it prevent the onset of the core symptoms of psychological problems and lead to greater quality of life? These questions bugged me relentlessly as I contemplated the possibility that so much suffering could be avoided.

Initially, my busy professional life carried on, but still this idea would not go away. The knowledge that proved so effective in the therapy room was being denied to the majority of the population who would never find themselves on a therapist's couch. What would happen if we routinely taught people to become effective self-managers of their mental health and wellbeing? Was broad psychological immunisation possible?

It was only when someone very close to me was seriously affected by mental ill-health that I was spurred into action. While I had always had empathy for my clients, seeing first-hand the devastation caused by a lack of these psychological skills affected me in a deeply personal way. Now I desperately wanted to know if it was possible to stop episodes of psychological disorders from occurring in the first place. Overnight, my intellectual curiosity and arm's-length theorising had turned into a personal and professional mission: to test and trial a new, skills-based approach to *preventive psychology*.

In society overall, there is a huge gulf in our general knowledge about building and maintaining our physical health compared to our mental health. We know to bend our knees when we lift heavy objects, we wear seatbelts to keep ourselves safe from physical injury in our travels, and we brush our teeth to prevent decay. Even if we don't always do what we *should* do to keep our bodies healthy, we at least have that basic knowledge. Yet our broader social consciousness seems to lack knowledge about protecting our mental health. It's as if we are experiencing the psychological equivalent of not brushing our teeth.

For the majority of people, if they made a New Year's resolution to become fit and healthy, or to complete a goal such as running a marathon, they would have a sense of the daily behaviours required to reach their goal. Whether they actually *do it* or not is an entirely different matter, but at least they would have some basic knowledge of what they should do.

But what if the New Year's resolution was to be as mentally healthy as possible, to develop a psychological edge to be at their best? My concern is that most people would be unaware of the daily behaviours required to get there.

Consider this. The type and strength of different emotions are central to our quality of life. Yet how many people do you think could give well-informed answers to the following questions?

- *Where do emotions come from?*
- *What's their purpose?*
- *How can I manage my emotions well?*
- *What does a healthy emotional life look like?*

Sadly, I think most people would struggle. Today's generation of young people was born into a world with a booming self-help industry and greater access to media and information than ever before. We are surrounded by buzzwords, good intentions, and awareness-raising. Political correctness, safe-spaces, and trigger-warnings abound. Diligent, protective parents raise their kids in an increasingly protected world. Yet our collective mental health has never been worse.

If, like me, you have grown frustrated with simplistic and clichéd recommendations to "think positive", "believe in yourself and you can do anything", or "just choose to be happy"; then you have probably been waiting for a more genuine, sophisticated, and realistic approach.

I have dedicated the past decade of my professional life to uncovering the core processes associated with mental health and wellbeing so we can rise above the tokenism and buzz-words to deliver truly effective psychological knowledge on a large scale.

I have reviewed over 700 research papers from around the world on what has and hasn't worked in preventing various mental disorders, and understanding how psychological problems develop. I have worked with thousands of young people teaching them sophisticated psychological skills and wellbeing strategies, and painstakingly assessed their mental health compared to control groups over time. My scientific research has been published in major international journals[1] and reflects the very latest developments in what we know about human psychology.

I have also learnt that when good psychological knowledge and a strategic focus on wellbeing is applied in a consistent, proactive way, it leads to peak performance. More than just preventing and overcoming problems, the principles of *being*

---

1 For example: Nehmy, T. & Wade, T. (2015). Reducing the onset of negative affect in adolescents: Evaluation of a perfectionism program in a universal prevention setting. *Behaviour Research and Therapy, 67*, 55-63.

well help us to *do* well. Enhanced energy, improved focus, healthier relationships, and a more clear, aware mind are just a few of many ways personal development creates a pathway to thriving. By taking powerful concepts out of the therapy room and systematically applying them for the purpose of personal growth, we open the door to higher functioning, broader horizons, and more exciting possibilities.

My personal mission now leads me to share the crucial insights I have gained over this long journey with you. Each chapter encapsulates steps you can take that have helped the thousands of people I've worked with to create emotional balance, peak performance, and lifelong wellbeing.

The keys to robust mental health and enduring high functioning are specific, repeatable, and can be readily applied in your own life, starting today. If you keep turning these pages and are willing to apply what you've learnt, I'll support you in creating a higher level of wellbeing to enjoy your best possible life.

CHAPTER 2

THERE ARE SIX KEY INGREDIENTS TO WELLBEING

WHEN PEOPLE SAY they want happiness, what they really mean is they want greater wellbeing. Our wellbeing is the baseline state of good functioning and contentment that we return to as we negotiate all the ups and downs of a worthwhile, interesting, and meaningful life. Unlike a focus on temporary mood states, wellbeing is more stable and broad, and creates the foundation for our quality of life. In this sense, being mentally healthy is about more than just your mind.

Worryingly, the field of personal development and our society as a whole is undergoing a popular revival of a dangerous concept: pursue good feelings and everything will work out fine. Feeling happy is promoted as the ultimate goal.

In the 1980's, society was swept up in the self-esteem movement which assumed that if we just praise people enough, they will feel good about themselves and therefore will feel happy and won't get depressed or encounter other psychological problems. But the self-esteem movement did not deliver the expected benefits because it didn't accept and deal with the reality that to be human is to be imperfect, that we all have strengths and weaknesses, and even people of good character and ability will sometimes make mistakes and perform poorly (and vice-versa).

This failure was made clear by subsequent rising rates of depression. If feel-good feedback was the key to sustainable happiness, shouldn't we have observed a decline in rates of depression? Some psychologists have argued that indiscriminate praise, which became particularly evident in parenting and the school environment, is one of the reasons depression rates rose: it created "learned helplessness". No matter what kids did, they got the same result. They were always told their performance or ability was wonderful, when inevitably, it wasn't always wonderful. This meant that kids lost a mechanism of reliable feedback from the authority figures in their lives that could help them identify their strengths and weaknesses, and learn how to deal with challenges effectively.

We have also since discovered that self-esteem is moderately correlated with narcissism. In the selfie-taking, social media world in which we now live, seeking positive feedback for temporary good feelings seems to be more a vicious cycle than a real solution to the desire for happiness.

More recently, a wave of "happyology" has proliferated not only in the personal development literature but also in parts of professional psychology and mainstream education. The word "positive" now seems to precede every noun, as if proclaiming something to be positive immediately sheds its negative aspects and magnifies its virtue. *Positive* psychology, *positive* education, *positive* workplaces, *positive* parenting.

Some aspects of these approaches have conferred benefit. But here again, good intentions have missed the mark: in wanting to discover more of something good we have rendered ourselves less able to deal with the reality of the wonderful but imperfect world around us. By focusing on generating good mood without teaching the specific skills of dealing with so-called "negative" emotions, this trend has alienated those people for whom positive emotions do not seem readily accessible. It has created an assumption (whether intended or not) that stronger and more enduring positive mood states are the hallmark of personal development success. Happiness is promoted as the end goal. Like an all-night party venue with buzzing neon lights, positive mood states should be open and available to us at any and all hours of the day, non-stop.

Ten Steps to Happiness!

Think positive and all your dreams will come true!

The alluring but deceptive premise is that 24/7 happiness is even possible. Being "up" in mood all the time is simply not how our brains are designed to work. The regular experience of good feelings is healthy and desirable, but emotions, by their very nature, are transient and temporary. If someone arrived in my practice and told me they feel up in mood all the time, I would think, *is this person experiencing a manic episode? Is this a drug psychosis? Do they have a serious neurological disorder?*

It's not normal to feel happy 24/7

The notion of feeling good all the time denies the reality that it is not normal to be happy 24/7. Emotions, by design, should be temporary and transient. The happyology approach implies that experiencing negative emotions means we're not there yet. We are somehow less than what we could or should be. But if feeling good is the end goal, then what about all the soul-testing journeys that make up a deeply purposeful, well-lived life but do not consist of abundant positive emotion?

In addition to being unrealistic and unnatural, perpetual good moods, like perpetual safety, would be boring and dull. Pursuing things that matter carries the hope of great rewards but also the risk of disappointment and loss. Anxiety and excitement are never far apart. This is the true yin and yang of our deep personal psychology, too easily glossed over when we pursue good feelings for feeling good's sake. As we are enriched by life's challenges and rewards, so too is the tapestry of our emotional lives woven together with varying and contrasting emotional states, as if from a vast palette of colours.

Real life includes both positives and negatives

Shit happens.

This crude, simple message was made into a bumper sticker because it's true. Unless we live cross-legged meditating in a cave, things will happen in daily life that challenge us and cause us discomfort. It is impossible to live a meaningful, fulfilling, and goal-directed life without experiencing some negative emotions. Life outside the cave means encountering challenging times that don't always feel good and circumstances over which we do not have total control.

But challenges aren't inherently bad. Being challenged just means *being taken out of our comfort zone.* A job promotion to a more demanding role might take us out of our comfort zone and is therefore challenging. Having to make a speech at a wedding might take us out of our comfort zone and be challenging. Likewise, losing a job and having to regroup and find other employment usually takes us out of our comfort zone, and is a confronting and challenging problem to overcome. None of these things is immediately conducive to feeling happy, yet they are each common occurrences that are important in that they can contribute to increased capability, enhanced relationships, or a better future. By successfully negotiating these challenges we can actually enhance our wellbeing and personal effectiveness.

Rather than working against us, circumstances that generate discomfort and occasional negative emotions are actually a vital part of learning and growth that we wouldn't want to be without. As I will present to you in this book, a good formula for personal development is to be exposed to challenges that expand our comfort zones, and our personal capacity to deal with future challenges, in a *graded and gradual way.*

Profound personal growth requires both comfort and discomfort. Robust mental health requires both positive and negative emotions. And wellbeing provides the foundation and resources to make each of these possible.

You can create greater wellbeing

Being truly mentally healthy requires a focus on wellbeing— our broader biological, social *and* psychological health—as opposed to trying to capture and hold onto feeling states which by their very nature are temporary and transient.

Wellbeing is about more than just your mind. It is about more than just feeling good. Rather it is an holistic and integrated view of many important factors that collectively determine our level of functioning and quality of life.

Where many people see personal psychology as being intangible or some kind of genetic luck-of-the-draw, readers of this book will learn that mental health is no more esoteric than learning how to change the oil in your car: it usually involves a specific and logical set of steps that are learnable and repeatable.

A helpful way of thinking about wellbeing is the Healthy Minds Wellbeing Wheel.

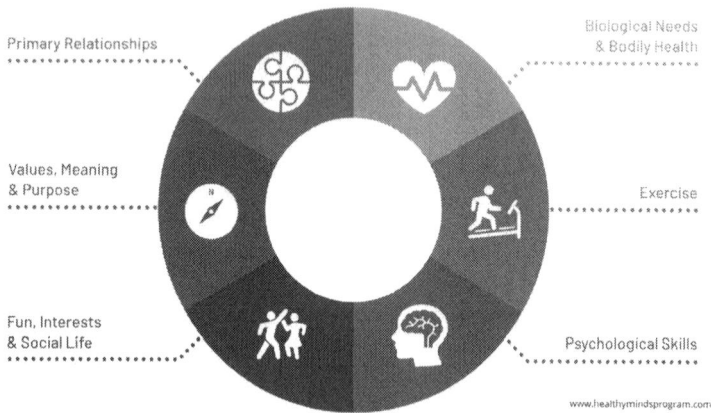

Take a look at the Wellbeing Wheel graphic above. Each segment is a major contributor to overall wellbeing. As we go around the wheel clockwise starting from the top left, consider what rating out of 10 you would give yourself for each of the wellbeing segments. At the end of this chapter, you will have a chance to rate and review each segment as it pertains to you right now.

Primary Relationships

The primary relationships segment refers to the people you live with, spend most of your time with, and/or who are closest to you in an emotional sense—for better or worse. Relationships provide a huge amount of context to our experiences of life, and influence our wellbeing greatly.

Mental health researchers generally look at three key factors in assessing wellness or disease: biological factors, psychological factors, and social factors. Each of these influence psychological outcomes greatly. This is known as the *bio-psycho-social* model. However, the *social* part of the biopsychosocial model is the one that tends to be under-emphasised. Key relationships have a significant bearing on our experience of everyday life.

So, what would a highly rated (healthy and fulfilled) primary relationships segment look like? It would mean the people we live with are people we get along with and preferably love and respect. The people we spend most of our time with in terms of family and close work colleagues would treat us well and these relationships would be largely free from major conflict. Ideally, all of those people we allow in our inner circle would treat us with kindness, acceptance, and compassion.

If you have a partner or spouse, this relationship will generally have a large impact on your wellbeing, especially if you live with them. But if your marriage is marred by conflict, jealousy, and distrust, then this will negatively affect your score.

If your work and personal relationships are generally great, that might feel like a 9, but if you cringe at the thought of going home to a conflictual relationship with your partner, that sounds like a 5, so maybe you'd go with a 7 overall. Get the picture? The specific number you end up with is subjective, which is totally fine because this is just for you and won't be used to compare yourself to others.

Biological Needs and Bodily Health

Our diet, the amount of sleep we get, consuming enough water and not too much caffeine or alcohol are essential aspects of wellbeing. On the extreme end, very poor diet or the excessive consumption of unhealthy foods and drinks will result in serious physical health problems including illness and chronic disease. Some people are also highly sensitive to foods such as sugar, caffeine, wheat, and dairy, and therefore experience mood swings, and peaks and troughs in their energy levels.

One of the most common deficits in this segment is a lack of water. Ensuring you limit your intake of sugary, caffeinated, or alcoholic drinks, and having plenty of water is a simple first step that most people could take to improve this segment. Not convinced that this will impact your wellbeing? Feel the difference in your alertness, energy levels, concentration and fatigue when you are hydrated versus dehydrated, and you will quickly see that this is an important factor.

You may want to include sex as a biological need in assessing this segment. For many people a satisfying sex life makes a significant positive difference to their mood, satisfaction, and stress levels.

If you have a healthy diet with no significant health issues you might want to score yourself a 9.5. But if you haven't had a check-up with your doctor in years or you're aware of a family history of cancer but have never done a screening test, you'll want to knock a couple of points off.

When assessing diet for this segment's score, keep in mind that healthy eating will contribute to a higher score, but *obsessive* healthy eating or calorie restriction is not ultimately healthy and will reduce your score. Overall, small improvements in habits such as sleep, diet, and regular health checks (for example) can have a big impact over time.

Exercise

Exercise gets a whole segment for itself. Why? Because it has such a big influence on mood management and stress relief. Research has found that for some people, vigorous exercise several times a week can have a major mood effect similar to or greater than that of antidepressant medications. It discharges stress, increases our physical capacity for daily life, and causes the release of endorphins that make us feel good. For any mildly depressed client I see, the first thing I usually get them to do is to increase their activity levels, and one great way to do this is to simply exercise.

When you assess your wellbeing related to exercise, think about how often you get your heart rate up. Do you walk or exercise regularly to a degree that gets you puffing? Is your fitness level functional? That is, are you able to do all the daily tasks in your life without excessive strain or fatigue? Exercise will also positively affect sleep, metabolism, and will lower risk for many potential health problems.

Psychological Skills

It is probably not surprising that the psychological skills segment is the one people find the most difficult to rate. The psychological skills that have a pervasive influence on our emotional lives are not commonly known and understood in the way bodily health factors (such as diet and exercise) are. On many occasions I have found myself sitting opposite a "stuck" client in my clinic, thinking to myself *unless this person found her way to my therapist's couch, what other opportunity would she have had to learn the psychological skills she needs?* The answer was "none". And herein lies the great opportunity we are now faced with: to identify the core sophisticated psychological skills we know help people greatly, and take them out of the therapy room and into schools, companies, and books to help as many people as possible learn how to manage their psychological wellbeing *before* they find themselves needing therapy.

The psychological skills I am referring to include concepts like helpful thinking, techniques for managing emotions, relating to ourselves in an encouraging and compassionate way, being flexible, understanding and prioritising personal values, being willing to tolerate discomfort, and more. The chapters that follow will teach you these concepts and how to simply and effectively apply them to your everyday life.

For now, give your rating based on your best impression of:

- How well do you manage strong emotions? Do you feel like you can make good decisions when having a strong emotional reaction to something? Do you find, in hindsight, that your responses fit the situation well or do you over- or under-react? Do you get stuck in states of negative emotion or do you tend to bounce back quickly?

- How accurate is your thinking? Do you tend to predict disaster that never seems to eventuate? Or do you under-estimate risk? Would your friends describe you as level-headed and flexible?

- How do you relate to yourself? Are you harsh and hard-hearted in your self-talk? Or are you an encouraging coach who employs constructive criticism but also acknowledges what you do well?

- How would you assess the quality of decisions you make? If someone was viewing your life as a movie, would they say you have navigated life well? Would they say have demonstrated an ability to learn from the past, and become wiser over time?

It doesn't matter if your rating feels like a guess—that's all it needs to be. Just by reading this book, your psychological skills segment will start to improve.

Fun, Interests, and Social Life

A healthy life is a balanced life. And no matter how driven or focused you are, part of being human is the need to take time away from work and goal-directed activities. We need to recuperate, focus on pleasurable things for their own sake, and enjoy social connections and activities.

Remember the "social" from the bio-psycho-social theory of wellness and disease? Apart from your primary relationships, this segment also nurtures that human need to feel connected to and supported by others.

If it feels like something's missing, if you'd like more social contact in your life, or you feel the need for a hobby or an interest outside of your usual work or family roles, your score will be lower. If you have all the social engagements you need, regularly engage in pleasurable activities, and have something that captures your imagination beyond the routine tasks of your life, then your score will be high.

Values, Meaning, and Purpose

In contrast to short-term aspects of wellbeing, which can be readily influenced by daily behaviour, is the big picture of our lives. This pertains to who we are, the roles we play, and why we are here. What gets you out of bed in the morning?

Your sense of purpose is the broader meaning with which you engage in life. Is it your work? Is it your role as a parent, grandparent, or caregiver? Or is it volunteering your time for a cause that goes beyond your own needs to give something back to society as a whole?

For some people, having a spiritual practice or religious belief-set provides a context that both soothes and drives them in their life's direction. Others might be driven by a large goal that they are working hard to bring to fruition. Whatever the cause, that sense of meaning and purpose, of striving for something of importance and relevance, is an essential component of overall wellbeing.

Likewise, living according to what we value is an intrinsic part of living in a purposeful way. Beyond enjoying good feelings, living according to your values provides a life rich in satisfaction and contentment that goes far beyond the pleasure of being comfortable, feeling happy, or leading a stress-free life.

Your score on this segment is likely to be low if life feels rudderless and you lack any motivation. (But if that's the case, fear not! We will address this later in the book). Your score on this segment is likely to be high if you have an inner drive that compels you to keep going in spite of challenges and discomfort; if you feel you have a contribution to make to the lives of others, or a personal mission that is meaningful and satisfying for you; or if the things you devote most of your time and energy to are those things you deem most important.

To Do and Digest

Rate your wellbeing on each of the six Wellbeing Wheel segments below. It doesn't matter if your rating feels like a guess. As long as you can get a sense of the relative strength of your six wellbeing factors this exercise will work well.

My Primary Relationships score is _____
My Biological Needs and Health Status score is _____
My Exercise score is _____
My Psychological Skills score is _____
My Fun, Interests, & Social Life score is _____
My Meaning, Purpose, & Values score is _____

What to do with your score

Once you've rated each segment around the Wellbeing Wheel, take a look at the scores in relation to each other. Which segment is your strongest? Which is your least strong? Have a think about your less well-developed segments and try to come up with 3 specific strategies to enhance your number on those segments. That is, 3 practical things you can *do* that are likely to cause you to score higher on those segments in a couple of weeks or a month's time. It is totally open-ended, the sky's the limit. It could be anything that will enhance your score. Remember, you don't have to implement every action at once. Prioritize and pace yourself.

My 3 wellbeing enhancement strategies are:

1. _____

2. _____

3. _____

You could even make a note of strategies for each of the six wellbeing domains. Make sure at least one of the strategies is something relatively easy, something you could definitely do in the next week. This will help build momentum with some early success and get you in the groove of thinking about and taking action to support your Wellbeing Wheel on a day-to-day basis. Ultimately, the goal is for you to be an effective self-manager of your own wellbeing.

Tracking and maintaining your wellbeing

Regularly auditing your wellbeing with the Wellbeing Wheel is an essential practice to build and maintain your best life. I recommend monthly reviews as this allows some time to really shift the needle on one segment or another, and also allows for the fact that these segments are often relatively stable, and take time to change.

While small changes may seem imperceptible over a few hours or days, a shift of 2 or more (subjective) points across the whole wheel between one month and the next will result in an increased overall sense of health, contentment, and satisfaction with life. If someone had poorer wellbeing a year ago, and she was somehow able to compare her life as it was side-by-side with her life now, she would certainly be able to *feel* the difference. Not just in an emotional sense, or a physical sense, or even a social sense, but in a hard-to-define combination of *all of the above.*

The power of the Wellbeing Wheel is that it takes that elusive feeling and breaks it down into an understandable, subjectively measurable, and actionable set of components that we can consistently improve and maintain. It provides a pragmatic, broad, and integrated model of mental health that transcends a focus on short-term emotional states. It enables you to become an effective *self-manager* of your wellbeing. Ultimately, this is the foundation of your quality of life, and provides you with the inner resources to take on challenges, ride out difficulties, and enjoy successes.

While the weather of our emotional lives continues to move through, over, and around us in an exquisite, natural, and fluctuating way, our wellbeing provides a solid foundation upon which the joy of life and the fruit of success is built.

CHAPTER UPGRADE

Get your free Wellbeing Tracker &
Wellbeing Wheel poster at:

www.tomnehmy.com/applesupgrades

CHAPTER 3

BE COURAGEOUS, NOT PERFECT

Two concerned parents sat on the couch in my clinic, explaining their worries about their four-year-old son Jimmy.

"He won't draw or do colouring in," they said with a genuinely concerned look.

I was naturally curious because all the four-year-olds I knew loved colouring in. After some further questioning, I discovered that Jimmy was refusing to draw because he worried about not doing it "right" and colouring outside the lines. His concern over making a mistake was strong enough that it over-rode his natural, childlike instinct to experiment and have fun using coloured pencils. As benign as this problem seems, it belies a larger issue—unhelpful perfectionism—and one of the hallmarks of being afraid of making mistakes: not trying at all.

Thankfully, we were able to help Jimmy by coaching him to see how mistakes help us learn, and prompting him to try challenging things by rewarding him for the effort rather than the outcome. But imagine if we hadn't intervened and

Jimmy's perfectionist mindset had played out over the course of years? His unwillingness to go out of his comfort zone and face the possibility of mistakes and failure, if left unchecked, would have greatly stunted his development.

In the adult world, however, perfectionism is often worn as a badge of honour, as if relentlessly pursuing self-imposed high standards defines someone as better than everybody around them. Where perfectionism was once seen as the mindset of high-performers, it turns out that rather than propel your performance, it is more likely to inhibit it.

There is some upside to a small amount of perfectionism: focus, drive, the desire to set goals, order, and organisation. All of these things come under the banner of "healthy achievement striving" and are generally helpful. But when striving to achieve gets too strong, especially if it's combined with fear of making mistakes, it gets in the way of both achievement and wellbeing.

Like four-year-old Jimmy, unhelpful perfectionism will often drive people to opt out rather than do a less-than-perfect job. They're more likely to give up when the going gets tough rather than persevere. Or they can take on so many tasks and goals that they become overburdened and over-stressed. Perfectionists take too long on tasks, see failures as disasters, become hyper-critical of themselves and others if things don't go according to plan, and are often shy of seeking feedback lest it damage their achievement-based sense of self-worth.

Joanna came to see me for stress and anxiety in her final year of high school. She was a naturally talented student who was sitting on a straight 'A' average across all her subjects. Unlike many of her peers, academic success had always come naturally for her. Yet now she found herself struggling.

Joanna's grades were starting to slip and she found it hard to get to sleep. She reported feeling lonely, stressed and anxious, and was concerned that her final year of high school was about to collapse around her. She started questioning her ability to complete assignments and was procrastinating, wanting to avoid handing them up at all.

When Joanna described her successes throughout school, she recounted having more badges for extra-curricular activities than any other student. Her badge collection included one for making the swimming team.

"But I *hate* swimming!" she said with an exhausted stare.

Like many perfectionists, Joanna's sense of self-worth was completely tied up in her achievements. Winning, getting top grades, and being the "best" had consumed her to the point that other important aspects of her life had come to suffer. She did what she hated in order to achieve. And now her wellbeing was in a steep decline.

It was only by letting go of her extreme perfectionism, and emphasising values other than achievement, that Joanna was able to relax a little and find a greater state of balance. Ironically, when she embraced this more flexible and less intense, less driven mindset, her academic performance actually increased. She finished the year as valedictorian of her school.

De-mythologising success

Because they fear mistakes and failures, perfectionists are highly driven to win and succeed. But this fear-driven motivation means they either stay only within those areas of achievement in which they feel confident of success, or they feel overwhelmed with pressure if facing a task that stretches their natural ability level. They will often give up easily. Or they won't try at all.

At the heart of unhelpful perfectionism is an exaggerated concern over making mistakes. Yet this denies the reality that we can only become competent at a new and challenging thing if we are willing to make novice-level mistakes first. As Dr Tal Ben-Shahar says in his book *The Pursuit of Perfect*, "We learn to walk by falling, to talk by babbling, to shoot a basket by missing, and to colour the inside of a square by scribbling outside the box."

Jaws and *ET* fans might not know that Steven Spielberg was rejected from film school three times, that Elvis Presley was told after his first performance to "go back to driving a truck", or that Stephen King's novel *Carrie* was rejected by 30 publishers. What each of these people had in common was not a perfectly smooth road to success, but a determined persistence in the face of negative feedback or outcomes. If they had suffered from unhelpful perfectionism rather than healthy achievement striving, the world could have been denied the fruit of their talents. Their efforts were fuelled by passion, and it seems their deeply held values drove them more than any fear of rejection or failure.

Invariably, successful people do not succeed on natural talent alone. They refuse to be deterred by negative feedback and are adaptable. They persist, despite multiple failures, by prioritising their drive to fulfil a closely held mission.

How perfectionism gets in the way

When I was doing my scientific detective-work in developing the program *Healthy Minds*, I had to look at the major risk factors for psychological problems in order to make my program as effective as possible. Those risk factors that were common to multiple psychological problems were the most compelling, because if I could formulate a program based on the antidote to these broad characteristics, my program would be more efficient. After reviewing hundreds of research papers, it became clear that unhelpful (extreme) perfectionism is a risk factor for depression, anxiety, and eating disorders. And rather than drive achievement, it gets in the way of peak performance.

Perfectionism is associated with some significant psychological pitfalls:

- black-or-white thinking,

- a self-critical style of self-talk,

- feelings of inadequacy, of never being good enough,

- not being able to enjoy successes as much as a non-perfectionist,

- a fear of taking risks, and

- an obsessive focus on failures.

Perfectionists will often take too long on tasks, avoid them, or see any minor imperfection as a major disaster requiring correction. Re-working and editing drafts of work well after the law of diminishing returns has kicked in becomes their standard *modus operandi*. Hyper-competitiveness and a win-at-all-costs mentality can put others offside. Sleep, effective time-management, and all the other important things in life included in the segments of the Wellbeing Wheel, fall by the wayside in preference of meeting those self-imposed high standards.

Do you want a perfect life, or an authentic life?

If we strive for perfection or seek to perpetuate an image of being perfect, we are choosing to shun our humanity. We are rejecting the one thing that connects us to every other individual on the planet: our imperfect nature.

Since there cannot be any growth without flaws and challenges, and any honest self-evaluation must accept that we have flaws or less-well-developed strengths, the myth of perfectionism renders us separate from our fellow human beings. In doing so, it actually limits our ability to relate to, and exist, within this human, imperfect world.

An authentic life is one that does not waste energy denying the existence of flaws and mistakes, which are part of our human nature. We can strive to iron out our flaws and learn from our mistakes, but to shun their very existence is disingenuous.

When we allow ourselves to be authentic, we reclaim all the energy and time spent trying to meet unrealistic expectations or uphold a particular image. The most devastating trap of perfectionism is that it does not allow us to fully live in each precious moment, enjoying the experience of being present with the magical and imperfect gifts that exist here and now.

An authentic and effective life requires a willingness to accept reality. The relentless pursuit of perfection (in how we look, the image we portray on social media, our income, job, friends, or mood) distracts us from what really matters. Rather than spending an extra three hours on a one-hour task, we would be better served getting on to the next item on the to-do list, getting to bed earlier, or spending time with family and friends. Instead of choosing only those contests we feel confident we can win, taking a chance on new and unfamiliar challenges expands our horizons and our comfort zones. Instead of sitting out of karaoke because we don't have a fabulous singing voice, we'd have more enjoyment if we focused on being silly and having fun for fun's sake.

Overcoming perfectionism

To overcome perfectionism, first look for growth lessons. If something doesn't go according to plan, ask yourself "what did I learn?" Only by facing challenges, stretching our boundaries, being tested and surprised, can we build our capacity to handle challenges in the future. These experiences are the building blocks of character and help us learn to do difficult things. A life free of any stress and discomfort is also a life devoid of personal growth.

Of the imperfections, mistakes, and failures you have faced, whether they were situations you willingly took on or from life circumstances that fate imposed on you, look for the part of that experience that enriched you. Regardless of the outcome: what was the gift of that experience? There is always a gift, if you will look for it.

If you are aware of perfectionism in one area of your life, say work relationships or housekeeping, try to find a *good enough* standard that meets the aim of your task but doesn't detract from other important things or negatively affect your wellbeing.

If you take too long on tasks, limit yourself to a reasonable amount of time. You could ask several other people how long they dedicate to that task, and then take an average as a guide.

Emphasise values other than achievement. What else makes someone a worthwhile person? What else do you think is important in life?

Embrace uncertainty and difficulty. The perfectionist mindset wants everything to go according to plan, but real life often does not go according to plan. The courage to embrace uncertainty and difficulty is necessary for anyone who aims to do great things. How many important things in the world would have occurred if everyone stayed within the range of what felt comfortable? No truly great or daring achievement has occurred in the absence of courage and flexibility.

Sustainable peak performance in any field requires that we let go of perfectionism in exchange for courage. Whether a world leader, a sportsperson, a CEO, or simply an individual trying to live a worthwhile life that contributes to those around them, courage means being willing to sometimes feel uncomfortable, to be exposed, to be less than perfect, and is therefore an essential stepping stone to a greater life.

To Digest

Unhelpful perfectionism is more intense and rigid than healthy achievement striving. It gets in the way of both achievement and wellbeing. Great strides in personal development can be made when we see the value in mistakes, challenges, and failures, and when we cultivate the ability to tolerate uncertainty and discomfort in aid of what we most value. Courage, flexibility, and authenticity are part of a healthy mindset that holds growth and learning, rather than achieving, as the most important outcome.

CHAPTER 4

EMOTIONS ARE NATURAL AND ARE DESIGNED TO HELP US

A DISHEVELLED MAN wearing a dirty trench coat entered the Blockbuster video store just before closing time. I was keen to get out of work as soon as my shift finished, distracted by my university assignment due early the next morning, so I didn't pay him as much attention as I probably should have until he set his umbrella on the counter.

Then I realised it wasn't an umbrella. It was a gun.

I froze. That's when I finally looked at our last customer of the day. His baseball cap was pulled down low over his head, revealing only a stubbly beard. My co-worker Adrian, who had been crouching next to me sorting returned movies in the drop box, stood and turned around to catch on to the situation just in time.

"Gimme your cash," the gunman growled.

Adrian and I could be moments away from being blown to pieces. Adrenaline burst through my body. My brain went into over-drive out of fear. I had to make some good decisions, and fast, if I was going to survive this.

Blockbuster's armed hold-up protocol led me to turn my back to the robber with my hands in the air. I shuffled to the side to reveal my empty till (I had already cashed up for the night because it was almost closing time). Adrian now had the tricky job of opening his till under pressure (it required typing in a password) and placing the cash drawer on the counter. Then he too turned his back to the gunman.

Seconds felt like minutes as we heard the gunman rummaging through the bank notes and coins, then:

Bang!

I hit the floor before I even had time to consciously register that the gun had gone off. The large glass shopfront windows shook violently from the shockwave. Frozen on the floor, I waited for what seemed an eternity before raising my head to see that the robber had fled the store. Convinced Adrian would by lying in a pool of blood, I was amazed to see his face with the same, bewildered look I must have had. He was convinced *I* had been shot. Somehow, we both escaped unharmed and quickly clicked into gear to lock the doors, activate the hold-up alarm, and call the police.

Fear had been my friend. The surge of adrenaline brought the world into sharp focus. It energised my brain and body. This energy helped me respond to a dire situation with urgency. The instinctive ducking for cover and covering my head with my hands when the gun went off did not involve making a choice, but it served to protect me from harm.

Emotions serve a purpose

Humankind today is a representation of what worked in the past. We are a reflection of what helped us survive. Evolutionary theory tells us that throughout the ages, the aspects of our bodies and brains that conferred an advantage were retained within the human genome. Things that rendered us less able to succeed in a primal, unforgiving world tended to fade out through the process of natural selection.

Just like advantageous physical capabilities have shaped the body though natural selection, so too have certain psychological and behavioural qualities, including the emotional centres of the human brain.

The starkest illustration of emotional adaptation is:

What would have happened to us if
we could not experience fear?

If we could not perceive and respond to threats effectively, if the links between emotions, brain processes, and the adrenal system did not work as they do, the human species would not have survived to be here today. This is why so-called "negative" emotions don't deserve their reputation.

It's normal that we don't want to feel unpleasant feelings, but they are not inherently bad. Fear, anger, and sadness are all functional. As uncomfortable as they can be, we would definitely *not* want to completely rid ourselves of them.

Positive emotions make us want to do more of what feels good. The pleasure we feel reinforces behaviours that supported evolution: companionship, sex, satisfying hunger.

Because positive emotions are inherently pleasurable, their presence in our lives is rarely questioned.

Our ability to feel the whole range of emotions is essential. Negative emotions have value because they urge us to behave in ways that can protect us. The quick-and-dirty instincts of the emotional brain helped us in the life-or-death existence of earlier times. But in the modern world, the context in which we respond is vital in determining if the urge is actually helpful or not.

Thankfully, since these primal beginnings we have also evolved a more complex part of the brain responsible for sophisticated and considered reasoning, planning, and judgment. Sometimes referred to as the thinking brain, it helps us make good choices in the modern world. But the more primal emotional brain retains its influence. Centuries on, these hard-wired emotional brain systems still send us urges to react in the heat of the moment. In the modern world, emotional reaction urges do not always serve us well. But their origin is one of instinct and survival, which is how they are best understood.

Emotions give us urges to react

Beyond the subjective, intangible feeling of an emotion is the real-world translation of that feeling into behaviour. An emotional reaction urge is what an emotion makes you want to *do*. Not only have reaction urges played a crucial role in the survival and evolution of our species, they still impact us today. Let's take a look at how negative emotions and their reaction urges can be helpful.

The Usefulness of Fear

Fear is our guardian instinct. In the earlier stages of human evolution there were many more mortal threats in the environment. The surge of adrenaline we get when danger is present helps keep us alive because it moves blood quickly to our arms and legs to help us move if we need to; our pupils dilate to enable us to clearly see the environment around us, and our breathing deepens to oxygenate the blood and prepare ourselves for action. If we did not have the capacity to feel fear we would not have been given the urge to run and hide to avoid these dangers, and would have been gravely vulnerable.

Had I not had the capacity to experience fear, I would have been at far greater risk of being shot during the video-store hold-up. For the successful evolution of the human species as well as the successful growth and survival of each person reading this book, fear and its associated urges has played a vital role. We owe our very presence, here and now, to our human brain's emotional centre providing us with the emotion of fear. The adaptive emotional reaction urge of fear is to *escape or avoid.*

The Usefulness of Anger

Anger is our defensive instinct and motivates us to seek justice. Historically, if we were threatened or intruded upon, we needed anger to help us defend our family, clan or tribe. In the modern world it gives us energy to defend ourselves and our loved ones, and to have the courage to fight when something is worth fighting for. Anger provides that impetus to override meekness and manners when we have been wronged and need to confront the situation. All of our social instincts urge us to get along, but when we need the strength to have a difficult conversation, to challenge authority, or to wade into a fight because diplomacy has expired and fighting is our only remaining option, then anger serves our purpose. The primal instinct to lash out in anger can fuel a last-line defence against physical threat. From an evolutionary standpoint, if we didn't have the surge of energy that anger provides, we would be less likely to overcome these threats, and less likely to survive. The adaptive emotional reaction urge of anger is to *confront or lash out*.

The Usefulness of Sadness

Sadness is our reflective, safety-seeking instinct. It provides the opportunity to examine a hurtful situation in order to avoid its recurrence. It slows us down to heal and recover from painful experiences. And when we are so afflicted by sadness that we cannot function, our visible malaise affords us the role of someone who is unwell, and helps absolve us of the responsibilities that are simply too much at that point in time. Sadness also prompts us to reflect on the good things we yearn for and to appreciate what we've lost. In early times, when we were feeling down as a result of deep sadness or loss and we couldn't muster the energy for daily tasks or we weren't thinking straight, being back in the cave was much safer than roaming, hunting or exploring. The adaptive emotional reaction urge to sadness and low mood is to *withdraw*.

The usefulness of fear, anger, sadness, and even other emotions such as envy, disgust, and surprise, have evolved as part of humankind because in some way they provided a survival advantage. In the modern world, negative emotions tend to get a lot of attention because although we need them, *we don't like the way they feel.*

Emotional systems are imperfect

Reaction urges are the crucial benefit of emotions, but they also pose a problem.

While escaping danger is the benefit of fear's reaction urge, escaping giving a presentation at work is not helpful. The fear of making a mistake or being embarrassed in front of colleagues and friends does not put us in physical danger but it causes a fear response nonetheless. The perceived social threat (goofing up the presentation) is responded to by the primal emotional brain in a similar way to an *actual* threat.

If tempered in the right way, the courage to stand up to a bully can be a benefit of anger's reaction urge to lash out. But lashing out at the office photocopier because it keeps printing your overdue report with blurry lines could get you into trouble.

Withdrawal and reflection for a period of time might help us to adjust after the loss of a relationship and the sadness that results. But ongoing withdrawal from activity and social connections is further isolating and depressing.

Ultimately, the survival advantage from emotional reaction urges that assisted early humankind must be tempered in the modern world if they are to be a helping rather than hindering force in our lives. The evolution of the thinking brain allows us to cultivate more nuanced responses based on self-control, reasoning, and good judgement. Herein lies the benefit of a truly integrated emotional system: going with reaction urges when they help, and resisting when they do not.

Which brings us to the ultimate psychological skill of all: making good decisions.

To Digest

Be willing to accept negative emotions. By understanding that there is a benevolent purpose to all feelings and that this is how nature intended us to be, we are less likely to be intimidated by, or afraid of, strong negative emotions. If we see negative emotions as bad or always as a sign that something is wrong, we invite a compounding of negative emotion. If we instead willingly and gratefully receive the message while reserving the right to contradict the message whenever it is appropriate and possible to do so, we create a firm bedrock for skilled emotion regulation.

CHAPTER 5

E MOTIONS DON'T CONTROL YOUR BEHAVIOUR, YOUR CHOICES DO

EIGHT-YEAR-OLD ROGER WAS on the brink of expulsion from school. I actually found him to be a very pleasant kid, despite the prophecies of doom that came through on his referral form, specifying numerous incidents in which he was the aggressor toward his third-grade classmates.

Roger had a strong sense of justice and was quick to stick up for his mates in the schoolyard. He was also a hothead. When he got angry, he didn't apply reason. Despite usually being well intentioned, his behaviour was regarded by his teachers as misguided, irresponsible, and sometimes violent. Rather than consider the consequences (detention, suspension, referral to me), he went with his primal urge. In the heat of the moment he couldn't see any alternatives, and his dominant response was to lash out.

We might like to think we have no choice in the matter when we are being reactive. The reality, however, is that truly uncontrolled reactions are a small minority of our behaviours. Think of a cook recoiling in a flash from touching a gas flame. Or the driver hitting the brake pedal before even consciously noticing the skateboarder who appears right in front of the car. Most of the time, however, we *do* have choices: the question is whether or not we engage in the type of thinking that brings those choices into awareness.

Behaving without being consciously aware of our thinking is called *automatic processing*. I refer to it simply as being on autopilot: engaging in instinctive or habitual responses without choosing between alternative options. Roger was so used to lashing out that he didn't perceive any alternatives to his aggressive reaction.

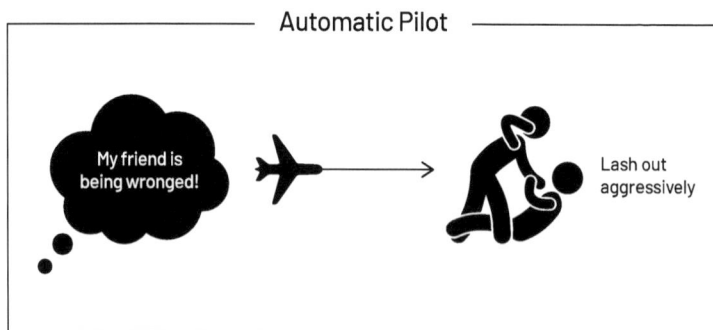

One key strategy I employed with Roger was to identify when his emotions were starting to run high—say, a 6 or 7 out of 10. Because strong emotions or stress make us more likely to operate on autopilot, I wanted Roger to be able to notice his anger rising. I asked his mother to help him note each day the situations that got him riled up. They would record the various triggers to get a sense of his different levels of anger and to become more aware of when he was entering these scenarios.

When he got good at identifying strong feelings, we needed to get him into the habit of noticing these *as they were happening* and then asking himself a question. This would require considering and selecting an answer from several options, which would pull Roger off autopilot and into the realm of conscious evaluation of his behaviour, known as *controlled processing.*

But which question should he ask?

The Magic Question

If Roger could ask himself the Magic Question right as he felt a strong reaction urge to lash out, he could switch off the autopilot that so often got him into trouble, and he would be in charge of what happened next. What's the Magic Question you ask? The Magic Question is:

What is the helpful thing to do now?

When on autopilot we only ever have one option, the dominant (most common, habitual or primal) response. The Magic Question or something similar, like "what are my options here?" takes us off autopilot and into the realm of controlled processing and mindful awareness. It provides a menu of choices that we can then consider in terms of *helpfulness.* Many of the decisions we later regret are based on what habit tells us to do, what emotion tells us to do, or what our peers tell us to do. Helpfulness, on the other hand, is a fairly good criterion by which to measure our choices.

The Magic Question – A List Of Options

My friend is being wronged! → What is the helpful thing to do now?

1 Lash out aggressively

2 Tell a teacher

3 Take my friend away from the bully

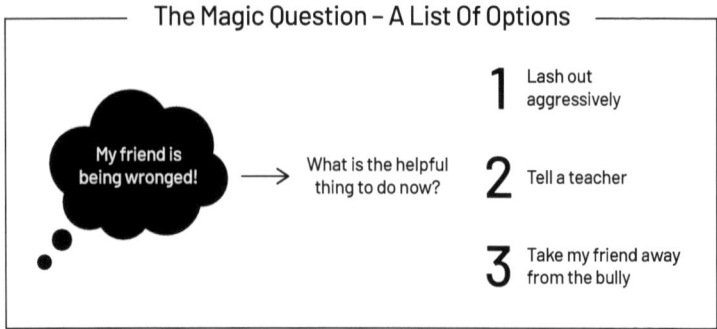

It's not guaranteed that we will follow through on the most helpful choice. But at least we have the opportunity to make a helpful choice when we pause to consider our options. With daily reminders and practice, Roger was able to rein in his unhelpful impulses, be more mindful of options and consequences, and make better decisions about how to handle conflict at school.

Like Roger, we in the adult world face the consequences of an autopilot response on a daily basis. We might yell at the kids when the TV is too loud on a Sunday morning. We avoid talking to a colleague because he is socially awkward, but whose friendship and cooperation might make work life go much more smoothly. We might habitually opt for the couch on a cold winter's night, when if we reflected on it, a fitness class is the thing we most urgently need to help our mental and physical health.

Here's another example of this process in action:

Your job is demanding, and every day, even though you can't wait to get home, when you do you snap at someone you love. Your kids rush the door, shouting their news at you. Your spouse is vacuuming or banging pots and pans around in the kitchen. You just want to get inside, take your business attire off, and sit down somewhere quiet to help you transition. When you're confronted with the shouting and the noise, you get irritated and snap at your family.

Next time you pull into the driveway, sit in the car for a minute. Imagine the kids and the spouse greeting you as they normally do. Now ask yourself, what is the most helpful thing I can do?

Option 1: Snap at the kids.

Option 2: Yell over the vacuum.

Option 3: Walk around the block to get my moment of quiet before going inside.

Option 4: Go in and ask the kids and my spouse if the family can make a new routine, one that allows you to enter a quiet house, take a few minutes to change clothes and relax, and then to re-emerge happy and ready for family time.

An option outside conscious awareness is tantamount to no option at all. The Magic Question deserves its name because it creates alternative behaviours and therefore alternative outcomes to problem situations where before there were none.

To Do

You too can harness the power of the Magic Question!

1. Identify the reaction urge that you struggle with the most. Is it avoiding the part of your job that makes you anxious? Is it taming your frustration with the kids? Is it getting to the gym when you're feeling flat?

2. Zero in on the most common situation in which this challenge arises. Visualise it and become very clear in your mind about when and where this choice-point is likely to occur. Is it before a staff meeting? Is it getting home after work? Make a mental note of this situation, and every time you enter the situation, use it to signal use of the Magic Question. Heck, set a reminder in your phone if you have to!

3. Practice asking yourself the Magic Question when this situation and reaction urge arise. By regularly asking yourself the Magic Question and following through on the best possible response from the options generated, you will have unlocked the power of your greatest emotional management tool: making good decisions.

4. Once you've identified the best option, you simply need to act on it.

Getting good at asking the Magic Question and identifying the best answer is a potent psychological skill that will enhance your wellbeing and your life. While it is a simple strategy, following through on the helpful choice is not always easy. To get the full benefit of the Magic Question, we need another tool in your toolkit: psychological muscle. If the Magic Question opens the door to helpful behaviours, psychological muscle helps you walk right through.

CHAPTER 6

PSYCHOLOGICAL MUSCLE IS THE FOUNDATION OF SELF-CONTROL

HISTORY PROVIDES MANY examples of those who couldn't restrain their impulses when emotional. From Ivan the Terrible, the Russian conqueror who killed his son in a fit of rage, to tennis ace John McEnroe, who was as well known for his tantrum-throwing as his tennis ability, those who are unable to engage their self-control and make a decision based on reason rather than emotion tend to end up on the wrong side of history.

We've probably all known someone who doesn't have much self-control in the face of emotional urges. Think of the acquaintance who rages at the slightest confrontation, such that a drive though the shopping centre carpark quickly descends into a red-faced fit of spittle and curse words, or the nervous workmate who seems to disappear every time a difficult meeting is scheduled.

Maybe even *you* could use more self-control in the face of emotional urges, especially those everyday situations that trigger anger or fear. Is it possible to feel irate at a rude driver and yet act in a calm way? Can you feel nervous as hell and still give the speech at a wedding? Can you push yourself to go out to lunch with your friends even if you woke up that morning feeling so flat you just wanted to pull the covers up? These are all examples of times when you would benefit from using psychological muscle.

The importance of psychological muscle

If the Magic Question provides us with options for how to respond to emotional situations, psychological muscle gives us the ability to follow through and exercise self-control in the face of strong reaction urges.

Individual reactions to emotions in our day-to-day lives may seem relatively insignificant. Who cares if we growl at our spouse after a stressful day? What's the matter with trying to get out of a tricky work task by taking sick leave? When taken on their own, these reactions seem without much consequence. But when they become part of a pattern of responding they add up to a significantly different psychological outcome. Every opportunity to view our options and choose a helpful response is a little fork in the road. Like turning left instead of right, we end up at a different destination and eventually we become a different person from the one we'd like to be.

Consider how the following examples might play out for someone who is ruled by emotional reaction urges:

30-year-old Stacey is in the early phases of a depressive episode that makes her want to withdraw. An old friend calls and asks her out for coffee.

What is her reaction urge telling her to do?

If Stacey just goes with her emotional reaction urge, will she go to the effort of dragging herself out of bed to meet her friend in a busy coffee-shop? She probably won't, and it will be to her detriment because being withdrawn and socially isolated for too long makes depression worse.

What would be the helpful thing to do?

The opposite of her reaction urge to withdraw is to *increase her activity levels.* By simply planning to do more, see friends, and exercise—precisely what her depression urge is telling her *not* to do—she would be giving herself the best chance of bouncing back quickly and returning to a healthy, normal range of mood fluctuations.

Jeff, a chronically stressed 45-year-old retail manager with a low level of wellbeing (remember the Wellbeing Wheel) gets told his second-in-charge just missed the deadline for ordering that week's stock.

What is his reaction urge telling him to do?

Jeff is at risk of losing his temper at his second in charge. If he gives in to the frustration-aggression he feels when he gets the news (something which is even more likely due to his chronic stress and low baseline level of wellbeing) he could alienate his staff and cause further problems in his workplace.

What is the most helpful thing to do?

The opposite of his reaction urge to lash out is to respond in a helpful, calm, thoughtful manner. By doing so, Jeff has a better chance of finding a solution while also maintaining harmony amongst the staff.

21-year-old Jenny is heading out to a friend's 21st birthday party. As she gets ready she feels the familiar sense of foreboding that usually accompanies social occasions. She is feeling butterflies in her stomach and her palms are becoming sweaty. As she walks up toward the entrance of the party house her anxiety starts to peak.

What is her reaction urge telling her to do?

Jenny's anxiety is producing a strong urge to go back to the car and text her friend with an excuse. If she leaves, she'll likely say to herself *thank God I left, I wouldn't have coped, and it would have been so embarrassing trying to talk to all those people I don't know. I would have made a fool of myself.* Jenny would then miss out on the opportunity to learn to cope better with social situations, and would be likely to believe her prediction for what might have happened rather than what would have actually happened.

What is the most helpful thing to do?

To help herself overcome her avoidance urge, she needs to do the opposite by seeking *exposure* to her feared situation.

Psychological muscle isn't just about being strong

Psychological muscle requires willpower, because we are actively resisting an urge. Like not having the extra piece of cake, we have to consciously decide not to do what comes more easily. It also requires mental effort to be consciously aware of and make an important choice. But sometimes people confuse building strong psychological muscle with being strong in a stoic sense. They assume it means we're denying the value of emotion, seeking to suppress the emotional brain, or suggesting it is better to be contained and unaffected when emotions arise. Psychological muscle is none of these things. Psychological muscle is about having the self-control to follow through on good decisions. And like the muscles in your body, you can build the strength of your emotional self-control with regular use over time.

It is easy to imagine the immediate benefits for Stacey, Jeff, and Jenny above if they make the most helpful choices. But building psychological muscle isn't *only* about immediate benefits; it's about long-term gains based on the cumulative effect of deciding to behave in the most helpful manner possible on an ongoing basis.

What kind of cumulative effects could Stacey, Jeff, and Jenny see over months and years?

For Stacey, it could be the difference between bouncing back from periodic low moods or a life of recurring depressive episodes. For Jeff, it could be the difference between climbing the corporate ladder or being limited to roles that don't require him to manage people. And for Jenny, it could be the difference between a life of connectedness and support or a life avoiding social interactions with others. For each of them the difference in their lives would significantly add to their overall quality of life and wellbeing.

Each of these people can secure the healthier, happier outcome by cultivating psychological muscle, and so can you!

A graded approach ensures success

If our most dreaded fear is a large birthday party with many people that we don't know, could we force ourselves to go? If we were the person feeling depressed, could we drag ourselves out of bed to meet a friend? Or confronted by a co-worker's mistake, could we follow through on the helpful, calm choice? Maybe.

But it may simply be too hard to immediately do the helpful alternate behaviours in the most difficult of situations. That is why it is necessary to build psychological muscle in a graded way. If the bustling and loud party with lots of strangers seems impossible, and the reaction urge to avoid the party is strong enough to drive you into a swarm of angry wasps, then we need to take a step back and engineer success with an easier challenge.

In the chapters that follow, we will look at graded ways to build psychological muscle for anxiety, anger, and low mood. But for now, one simple self-control task, practiced daily, is the place to start.

To Do and Digest

How to start developing your psychological muscle

Like doing weights at the gym, it takes time and self-discipline in a *repeated* and *graded* way to become fit and healthy in dealing with emotional urges. It isn't always easy to find that self-discipline, but it becomes easier to take on greater challenges if we consistently build our capacity over time. The best pathway to high levels of psychological muscle is to build momentum by regularly succeeding at small tests of self-control. As Naval Admiral William H. McRaven said in his inspiring speech to University of Texas students: "If you want to change the world, start off by making your bed."

Your mission is to choose a situation that requires you to exercise a *small amount* of self-control to over-ride a *small* urge. Try something easy. It might be taking a deep breath and putting a smile on your face before you walk through the door after a stressful day at work. Or over-riding the urge to press snooze on your alarm clock in the morning and getting out of bed the first time it goes off. Or deliberately saying "Good Morning" to the frosty colleague in the neighbouring cubicle when it's easier to give him a wide berth. You get the idea!

What you specifically choose to do is not especially important. What is important is that you accept a daily challenge that involves self-control and that you can *follow through on consistently*. If you can get seven days in a row, you will have made a great start. Keep it up for a month and you'll have great momentum. Eventually, if you keep succeeding at your self-control challenge behaviour, it will become a new normal.

Take back your power

When you develop strong psychological muscle, you are in charge of your reactions to life events no matter how challenging they may be. *You,* as opposed to your reaction urges, will determine whether you turn left or right at the junctures of life. Being able to follow through on the most helpful response, regardless of how you feel, will consistently lead to good outcomes.

The combination of the Magic Question (fostering awareness of helpful choices in the moment) and psychological muscle (having the thoughtful self-control to follow through on them) are the golden keys to life success. Even if you're in the most woeful of positions, there are helpful choices available to you *right now* that will improve your circumstances.

The martial arts parable of persistence says that if a student lays down one sheet of paper, it looks like nothing. But if every day he lays down a sheet of paper, it soon will amount to a great, formidable stack. If you lay down one piece of paper by way of exercising your psychological muscle each day, it might not seem like much in the moment. But if you keep going, soon enough you will have a stack of good outcomes sitting at your feet, and rising.

Even the most insidious psychological problems can be reversed with good decision making and self-control. The flipside of the problem becomes greater functioning, freedom, and effectiveness.

Let's start with the most common psychological problem of all: anxiety.

CHAPTER 7

ANXIETY CAN TURN INTO CALM AND CONFIDENCE

ANXIETY IS THE most common psychological problem there is. It disrupts people's personal and professional lives and saps their ability to function well. Instead of being able to enjoy the here-and-now, sufferers are continually distracted by the next (potential) disaster. Yet anxiety grows out of a very healthy and natural emotion that we absolutely would not want to get rid of: fear.

Anxiety is a misguided safety mechanism

We know that fear is a natural reaction to danger, and our brains and bodies are conspiring to *help us*. We *want* to experience the symphony of coordinated processes that help us to escape the burning building or jump out of the way of a speeding car. But what about when the fear response is activated without the presence of danger? What if our heart starts racing when we're about to go into a meeting at work?

Or we get the urge to flee before giving a "thank you" speech at a social club dinner?

The tricky thing about the human fear system is that it tends to respond to our *perception* of threat rather than the actual level of danger a situation poses. Avoiding or escaping a physically safe but challenging situation is the point at which helpful fear descends into a well-intentioned but meddling mess of reaction urges and safety-seeking. Psychologists use the term "safety behaviour" to denote something people do to increase their feelings of safety, but that actually work to maintain anxiety in the long run.

If I feel anxious in crowds and believe I always need someone with me when I go into a busy shopping mall to stop me from panicking, I will attribute staying calm to the presence of the other person and will come to rely on them. This in turn stops me from learning that I might be able to get through it on my own. I don't get to disprove my belief that I will panic if I go to the mall on my own, and without ever going to the mall on my own, I can't gradually develop the independence and confidence I need to overcome my anxiety.

Avoidance is the most common safety behaviour of all, but safety behaviours can take the form of many little reassurances that at best are passive and at worst are disruptive. Each safety behaviour is in response to a fear-based reaction urge but does not actually help us adapt to the challenge or threat we perceive.

Consider the following list:

Feared Outcome	Safety Behaviour to manage anxiety	Unintended Negative Consequence of the Safety behaviour	Prevents me from learning that...
Getting sick	Washing hands excessively	Cracked skin, greater risk of infection	Normal hand washing is effective at preventing disease
Being embarrassed in a social situation	Avoid social situations	Social isolation; reduced social skills; low mood	Most social situations are enjoyable
Not having anything to talk about	Prepare a list of discussion topics or questions	Come across as awkward and rehearsed	Spontaneous conversations are rewarding and interesting
Won't be able to find a toilet if I need one	Check where the bathroom is whenever I arrive at a new place	Takes up time, interrupts occasions	I won't wet myself even if I am unaware of the specific location of the bathrooms
My plane will crash	Avoid flying	Limits my experience of the world; can't go on overseas holidays	Flying on commercial airlines is safe

Feared Outcome	Safety Behaviour to manage anxiety	Unintended Negative Consequence of the Safety behaviour	Prevents me from learning that...
Feeling overwhelmed by a traumatic memory	Try to suppress thoughts of the event	Trying to suppress unwanted thoughts leads to having more of those thoughts	If I allow traumatic thoughts to come and go, I might not think about them as often

Safety behaviours mask the breakthrough

In essence, all safety behaviours are a type of avoidance: avoidance of something we believe we cannot cope with. The breakthrough moment for anyone who struggles with anxiety is when they truly understand the irony of this strategy. Avoidance of situations that are safe but make us feel anxious (as in our list above) deny us the opportunity to learn two important things: one, what would really happen; and two, when we face this type of discomfort, we will adjust and get through it.

Avoidance ensures that the anxious belief goes unchallenged, and so it lives on. We're then more likely to experience anxiety in the future, not less.

The alertness and bodily sensations that come from fear operate all the time on a small scale whenever we are out of our comfort zone or being challenged. We don't want to get rid of this natural ability that our brains and bodies have to keep us on our toes. But we mustn't catastrophise these feelings either. As you have learnt, the crucial juncture in dealing effectively with anxiety lies in making good decisions in response to the urge it presents.

Avoiding actual danger is a helpful response which keeps us safe.

Avoiding challenging or uncomfortable situations that are actually safe disrupts our life and holds us back.

Remember Jenny and her social anxiety from the previous chapter? We know she fears being embarrassed in a social situation, such as a birthday party where she won't know many people. By skipping the party, she won't learn that she could enjoy socializing with new people. And, crucially, her avoidance prevents her from learning that anxious feelings from the adrenaline rush of anxiety, including her racing heart and butterflies in her stomach, will not remain at an intense, uncomfortable level if she stays in the situation long enough for her body to adjust.

When using avoidance as a strategy to cope with anxious feelings, people do not learn the secret to overcoming them. That secret is *habituation*.

Exposure allows habituation

Habituation means getting used to situations so they no longer trigger such a strong reaction. It is the number one most powerful and reliable strategy for overcoming anxiety.

Anxious people can use their psychological muscle to overcome anxiety through the *repeated* and *prolonged* exposure to situations that make them feel anxious. Jenny could set herself the challenge of going to the birthday party. She might be able to force herself to go in the party to say "Happy Birthday" to her friend, but if she races out quickly and goes home after only a few minutes, she won't give herself time to adapt and adjust to this social experience. Escape is just as unhelpful as avoidance.

If Jenny does stay for the whole party, and we tapped her on the shoulder after mingling with other guests for 15 minutes or so, how do you think she would rate her anxiety out of ten? She might say that her discomfort has gone down from an 8 to a 6. If we asked her another 20 minutes after that? Maybe a 4. She will have habituated through *prolonged exposure*.

Prolonged exposure is like a hot bath

Jenny's body, like everyone's, has complex homeostatic mechanisms: processes designed to bring her bodily systems back into balance. These occur for temperature, adrenal releases (anxiety), the immune system, and many other hormonal and physiological processes that exist in the body. The bodily changes that come with strong anxiety such as a racing heart, feeling hot and sweaty, and butterflies in her tummy, can and will come back into balance if she allows herself the chance to adjust by staying in the situation long enough. In this sense exposure is like a hot bath. If we got into a hot tub on a cold winter's day, the first sensations are that it's too hot. But if we immerse ourselves and sit there long enough, our body adjusts and it becomes comfortable and enjoyable.

As the last guests shuffle out, Jenny leaves feeling tired but somewhat euphoric at having made it through the evening while also having fun and making new friends. If she is observant as she reflects on the night during the drive home, she would also realise she could learn three crucial things from her experience:

i. Her experience of emotion faded over time. The unpleasant bodily sensations that came along with her anxiety were brought back into balance as her adrenaline-fuelled fear response faded. From the time she walked in until the time she left her discomfort or distress reduced from 8/10 to 4/10, i.e. it *halved*.

ii. She learnt more about how to cope with social situations. By being on the ground in a busy, noisy social situation she was forced to speak to others, introduce herself, and engage in the usual chit-chat that goes along with meeting new people or catching up with old friends. This experience will make her better prepared for next time. Being out of her comfort zone here will help her tolerate this type of situation later.

iii. She learnt that her expectation for how the party would be was way off. She had imagined an embarrassing, panicked disaster, but instead she got through it ok and even managed to enjoy herself. The way reality played out did not reflect the inaccurate, anxious prediction she made which over-estimated the chances that something would go wrong and over-estimated how bad it would be if something did go wrong.

Has Jenny now overcome her social anxiety and developed enough psychological muscle to go to parties and chat to strangers with ease? Unfortunately, no. One workout isn't enough to be fit, remember? Exposure is effective when it is prolonged and also *repeated*. She should plan to repeat this process multiple times, until the initial emotion is much less. If she scheduled in a social event every night for three weeks, how anxious do you think she would feel walking up to the door on the last night of the third week? You guessed it, probably not very anxious anymore.

The anxiety you feel in your body, like sweaty palms or butterflies in your stomach, will go away if you give yourself time to adjust to the situation. The more often you give yourself the opportunity to experience your anxiety melting away, the quicker it will happen. The first time you give a presentation to your boss, you may feel nervous through most of the talk, but by the twentieth time, you probably won't feel nervous at all. Or if you do, you'll find yourself relaxed within a couple of minutes. Practice may not make it perfect, but it will make it easier.

Graded exposure is like steps on a ladder

Jenny's successful experience above would be a reasonable expectation for many people who wanted to face their similar fears. But what if Jenny's anxiety was *very strong*, and produced a reaction urge to avoid the party that her psychological muscle simply couldn't overcome?

She could make it easier using *graded* exposure. Jenny could construct an exposure hierarchy: a ladder of increasingly challenging tasks that bring her closer to her end goal of attending a crowded party. Instead of going headlong into the party, feeling overwhelmed and racing home in distress (which would reinforce her anxiety), stepping down a rung or two and starting with a smaller goal would make it manageable. She should start with something just one step outside her comfort zone, but that she could probably do if she pushed herself.

Graded Exposure

A large birthday party with lots of unfamiliar people

Going to a party with a mix of familiar and unfamiliar

A small group going out to lunch with several unfamiliar people

Meeting a familiar friend with someone new for coffee

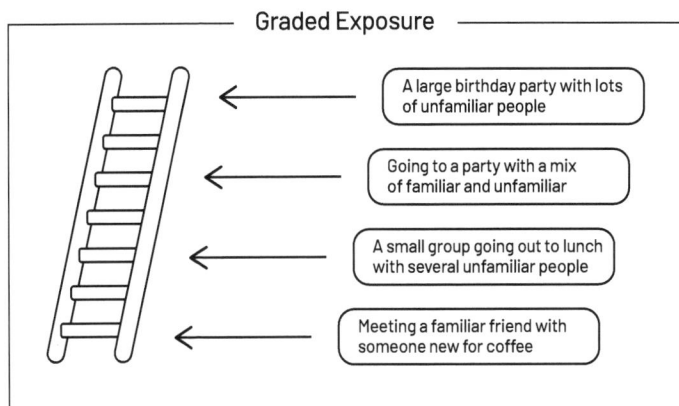

The simplified ladder above shows four steps, but if these jumps in difficulty seemed unmanageable, she could break the progression into 8 smaller steps, for example. The first step on her exposure ladder, meeting someone new in the company of a good friend over coffee, is something that would feel uncomfortable (say a 5 out of 10 on the discomfort scale), but it's not so great that she couldn't over-ride that feeling by using her psychological muscle, because she really wants to become more socially confident and competent.

Repetition builds momentum

One coffee date will not be enough to instil lasting change. Rather, Jenny should do this task *repeatedly* until she feels much less anxious at the prospect of a coffee date. In time, going out to have coffee with a friend and unfamiliar people will seem easy, and this is an indication that her comfort zone is expanding. For many anxious people and really anyone stuck in an emotional rut, their comfort zone will be a lot like a three-inch pizza: smaller than it should be, and not enough to sustain us!

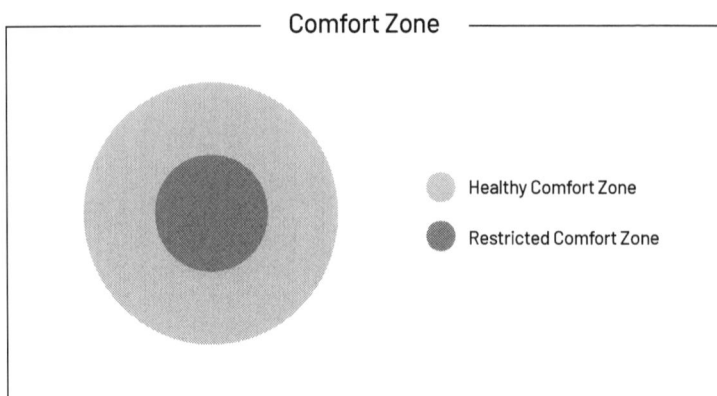

Comfort Zone

Healthy Comfort Zone

Restricted Comfort Zone

Expand your comfort zone in multiple contexts

By ensuring you do exposure tasks in many different contexts, your progress will also apply to many different situations. In the case of Jenny wanting to overcome her social anxiety, she would work through her exposure ladder for meeting unfamiliar people, ranging from easier scenarios right up to her most challenging goal: the big party. But Jenny also lacks confidence when talking to colleagues at work, particularly those in authority positions. She also struggles at family functions, where cousins and uncles keep teasing her for being too quiet. And finally, she is hopelessly anxious when faced with anything even resembling a romantic encounter. To really change her life, create some emotional balance, and improve her overall wellbeing, Jenny should take the step-by-step approach to exposure tasks in these four contexts. If she can steadily work toward her goals in each of these areas she will eventually find that very few situations faze her. Her calm and capability in these specific scenarios will eventually translate to a general, overall sense of being calmer and less anxious, no matter what she is doing. She will see progress in all areas of her life. If she limits her graded approach to one social situation, she will limit her progress to that one arena. It's like going to the gym and only visiting the treadmills, but never seeing the weight room or sauna or yoga mats.

Examine the figure below; it outlines four different contexts in which Jenny could tackle her anxiety and expand her comfort zone and capability.

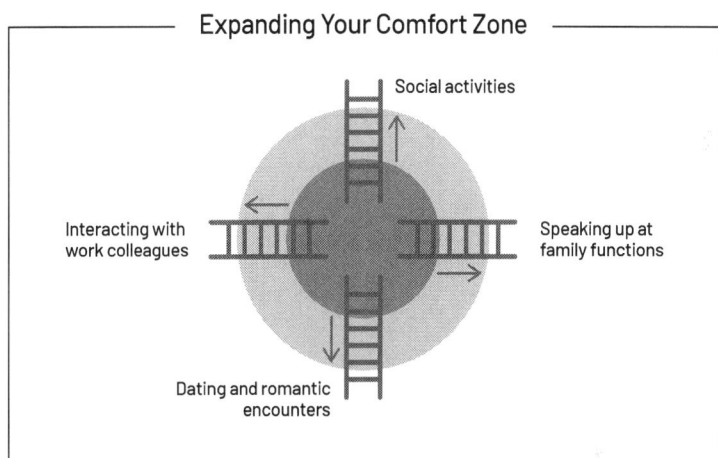

Expanding Your Comfort Zone

Social activities

Interacting with work colleagues

Speaking up at family functions

Dating and romantic encounters

Jenny is starting in the middle of the ring. As she climbs the steps of each ladder she expands that area of her comfort zone. When she has expanded her comfort zone in each area, she will have a full and balanced comfort zone for her whole life, not just the four situations in which she is challenging herself.

Not everyone will have multiple exposure targets. Some people simply have one very specific scenario that is their Achilles heel, in which case they need to focus only on that. But for those like Jenny who have several related contexts in which their anxiety rears its head, it is necessary to tackle at least several of these. Progress in several areas will generalise to all areas. The hope for anyone who feels consumed by anxiety in a hundred different situations is that you don't need a hundred exposure ladders! Pick the most disruptive few and watch as your overall confidence and psychological muscle grows.

Each of Jenny's contexts provide opportunities for repeated, graded, prolonged exposure. She must first determine the specific behaviours that are one step outside of her comfort zone for each of her work life, her social life, her family life, and her romantic life. She can then plan to complete personal missions *to do* the target behaviours on the first step of each ladder. She already knows she's going to feel uncomfortable doing them. She knows the familiar feeling of the reaction urge to escape or avoid. But having the courage to change your life means having the courage to experience discomfort or to make a mistake.

If Jenny persists, she *will* begin to feel comfortable entering these situations.

Doing, rather than avoiding social situations will become her new normal. Like water flowing down a new estuary these "new" confident behaviours will come naturally to her. When her comfort zone has expanded out to the first step on all four ladders, her experience will have generalised. She can reasonably be expected to handle similar situations in most or all contexts. She will have successfully pushed her comfort zone out one step all around the circle. If she keeps going in a persistent and systematic way, her ladders will all lead to an expanded, healthy comfort zone of a normal or even high-functioning person.

Although Jenny is required to willingly step into a state of discomfort, to activate her reaction urges and flight-or-flight response to some degree, it is not meant to be overwhelming. She can determine the pace at which she wants to proceed. The very idea of graded exposure is that it starts at just one step outside our comfort zone, the kind of challenge that we would normally tend to avoid but that we could probably do if we pushed ourselves. So while Jenny's exposure to social situations will make her feel uncomfortable, they shouldn't overwhelm her or make her panic. If that happens, it means the first step was a step too high, and she should think of something easier. Still outside her comfort zone, mind you, but not *terrifying*!

Our aim with any behavioural challenge is to ensure our discomfort goes down by about half in each exposure trial. For example, let's say I feel anxious in crowds and determine that walking through the shopping mall near my home would bring a discomfort score of 6/10. I accept that I will feel uncomfortable, including all the physiological sensations of anxiety (heart rate, sweaty palms, butterflies in my stomach, hot flushes). I know the reaction urge associated with anxiety is to escape or avoid but I will stay walking through the mall until my discomfort score is a 3/10 or less.

If I go walking in the mall each day, staying at the mall until my discomfort score halves, I will eventually notice my starting discomfort score is very low. A low discomfort score at the start of the challenge means success. My comfort zone for that situation has expanded to the first rung of the ladder. My next task is to simply move to the next step of the ladder, and repeat the process. If I am committed and consistent, the top rung of my ladder will eventually be just another step in my inevitable and natural progression.

Overcoming anxiety and building confidence use the same process

Whether overcoming a phobia or building confidence in a new area of life, the process is exactly the same. Each is a triumph of *willingness*: to exercise and build psychological muscle and to tolerate discomfort inherent in stretching the boundaries of your comfort zone. Never has a successful performer, businessperson or sports star felt completely comfortable all the time, especially when they were starting out or striving for a new and higher level of functioning.

If you can willingly face the well-intentioned but misguided manifestations of your fears and sit in the uncomfortably hot bath of your deepest goals, you too can release yourself from the chains of a fear-driven life and step confidently into higher levels of functioning.

In my work as a public speaker teaching these very skills and concepts in the *Healthy Minds* program, I am living this principle every day. From my first shaky, nerve-wracked attempt at a conference presentation to now regularly striding out in front of audiences of hundreds of people, I am living proof of how graded, repeated, prolonged exposure can turn nervousness and fear into alertness and focus, giving rise to an infinitely more exciting, more rewarding life.

To Do

Whether your goal is to overcome a fear, build your confidence, or achieve a new vision of success, you have the courage, will, and choice necessary to expand your comfort zone.

A blank ladder graphic is reproduced for you as a chapter upgrade (go to *www.tomnehmy.com/applesupgrades* to download). Use as many ladders as appropriate to your challenge or goal.

On the first rung of each ladder, describe the step you will take to expand your comfort zone. If you are very afraid of seeing the doctor, you might make the first step parking outside the doctor's office and sitting in your car until your feel calm. You will do this step enough times that it starts to feel comfortable. Then you can go to the second step.

On the second rung, describe the next step… you might enter the lobby and sit in the waiting room until you feel calm.

Keep going until you have a clear pathway to reach your goal.

No matter what the starting point, applying these principles enables each of us to foster the quiet courage to create confidence where we once had none, and calm where there once lived unnecessary fear. By embracing the challenge of careful and deliberate graded exposure toward our goal, we can build a personal capacity to be, do, and have more than an anxiety-driven life would allow. Suddenly, many previously unattainable things become possible.

CHAPTER UPGRADE

Get your exposure ladder template at:

www.tomnehmy.com/applesupgrades

CHAPTER 8

FRUSTRATION AND ANGER CAN BE HARNESSED

WHEN MY OLD school friend John gets angry, he goes all red. I half expect steam to appear from his ears like a cartoon character. It can be scary. Over the years I have witnessed John threaten someone while driving in his car, shove someone out of his way on the street, and scream at work colleagues with spittle flying out of his mouth.

On each occasion John felt entirely justified and showed no remorse.

The funny thing is, John can be a kind, generous, and empathic person, depending on the context. And he is not alone. Many people are generally kind, generous, and empathic, but their anger gets the better of them. We might describe them as having a short fuse or anger management issues or being hot tempered or quick to fly off the handle. The fact that we have so many colloquial ways to say someone gets angry is representative of how common an issue it is. Even those of us without an issue *per se* have at some time

or another lost our cool and maybe even suffered the consequences.

What John and people like him don't know (and what
I've never dared tell him) is that despite being a generally
good person, their psychological makeup contains a cocktail
of ingredients for problematic anger. By observing him over
many years I've come to notice that he:

- expects others to have hostile intentions,
- believes events are personal when they are not,
- filters out information that does not confirm his
  worldview, and
- has high levels of frustration with his own life.

What I want John and *everyone* to know is that regardless
of your current psychological makeup, you can harness anger
and reduce its negative consequences, like stress-related health
concerns, frequency of arguments, and workplace misunder-
standings. Anger is often a healthy and justified response to
life events, but when it occurs repeatedly in relatively benign
situations, it causes problems.

Let's look at each component of John's outlook to see
how his problematic anger could be overcome. Even if you
don't suffer from problematic anger, we all have moments of
temper when we might have been charitable. The lessons here
could benefit your life by helping you keep your cool under
pressure or better understand those around you.

Assuming hostile intent

When we assume hostile intent in others, we are primed for defensiveness and anger. When John drives, for example, he may appear calm on the outside, but he is a dormant road-rager who could explode at the slightest trigger. If he is driving along and someone cuts into his lane, he doesn't think *they made a mistake*, or *they didn't see me*; he thinks *they just tried to run me off the road!* This might sound unrealistic (and it is), but if you ask someone with chronic anger issues how confident they are in this kind of interpretation, they will often say "100%".

The assumption of hostile intent leaves no room for alternative explanations. It doesn't allow for the possibility that the offending driver couldn't see us because they had the sun in their eyes, that we were in their blind spot, or that they simply made a mistake. These other possibilities don't absolve the other person of any blame, but they don't contain the *intention* to do harm or cause inconvenience.

One of the less widely recognised causes of bullying behaviour is that it's a defensive action based on assuming hostile intent. Some bullies are simply mean, but others have been victims or see themselves as victims, and react in a pre-emptive manner to what they perceive as potential threats. Their extreme vigilance means they automatically perceive threats in ambiguous situations, and exaggerate the threat when there is one.

Overcoming the assumption of hostile intent relies on us putting ourselves in the other person's shoes. What if the bad driver was a good friend's elderly grandmother? Would we be so quick to blast our horn? What if he was racing home to his injured child? Remember that everyone has their own battles, we may not know what they are, and surely both we and those we meet will benefit from persistent kindness.

Looking for examples of our common humanity, our imperfect nature, allows room for other interpretations of people's actions. Have you ever clumsily bumped into someone while walking through a crowded bar? Or sent an overly-brief email reply because you were running out of time for a deadline? None of these actions is aggressive or provocative by nature, instead they are a result of human foibles.

If we give others the benefit of the doubt in ambiguous situations we will experience less conflict, face fewer confrontations, and can bounce back from these minor infringements without a lingering hostility.

Personalisation

Personalisation is the tendency to assume something is directly related to us when it is not. When John, for example, doesn't get a call back, he automatically thinks it's because they don't care, rather than because they have a lot going on in their life and forgot.

John teaches the guitar. If one of his students stops taking guitar lessons from him, he feels resentful of the time he has already invested in the student, rather than consider that it's their choice how they spend their time and money.

John's tendency to take things personally is another example of assumptions at work. He doesn't consider the other reasons behind the events that upset him. John's reaction doesn't mean he lacks all empathy, it's because he doesn't look for explanations from the other person's point of view.

Any time we feel miffed, rejected, or unfairly treated, personalisation can be overcome by writing down three other possible explanations for this event. Like the Magic Question, writing down possible alternative explanations gets our thinking off autopilot and into the realm of flexibility, shades of grey, and healthy doubt.

When you look for injustice, you will find it

The mantra John has repeated over the years in response to his perceived mistreatment by others is "people always disappoint me". Despite the many positive things that also occur in his life, John links all of the apparent injustices into a narrative that fuels his thinking. Known as *confirmation bias* (the tendency to pay attention to only those events that confirm our expectations), he focuses so much on events that confirm his outlook that he misses the many examples of kindness, forgiveness, and tolerance that could balance out his worldview. If he looked for those, his simmering anger would have a chance to truly settle.

Problematic anger is a vicious cycle: looking for hostile intent breeds hostility within. Could the reverse also be true? Looking for the good or benign intentions of others, acknowledging human frailties, seeking out examples of kindness, and practising the humility to admit our own shortcomings are all strategies for breaking the cycle.

Channelling emotional energy into action

One of the upsides of frustration and anger is that it comes with an impetus to act. Even when misguided, the reaction urge of lashing out is designed to right a perceived wrong and to protect. Anger's aim is to seek justice. That energy just needs to be channelled in the right way.

What if the emotional energy bubbling underneath John's surface was directed into a determination to improve his life? When his anger flares up, his wellbeing is also invariably low. Had he taken that frustration and used it as motivation to throw himself into addressing whatever deficits were present in his Wellbeing Wheel, he could have naturally improved his capacity to deal with whatever challenges he encountered. When our wellbeing is high, we have more internal resources: more patience, clearer thought, and a calmer spirit.

Interpersonal success involves seeing the best in others

Skilful leaders draw out people's strengths and make them feel good about themselves, even if they share a different opinion or value set. They find a way to validate another person's point of view even if they don't agree with it. As a result, they are more respected, better liked, and have greater influence.

Many conflicts are not the result of differing goals but differing views of how to get there. Interpersonal influence at its most powerful transforms opposing someone to sitting alongside them. And it is hard to sit alongside someone when you assume the worst in them.

The opposite of assuming hostile intent is recognising that others are doing their best. This doesn't mean being a pushover or foregoing all boundaries, but acknowledging others' efforts and good intentions regardless of the outcome.

To Do and Digest

If you ever feel like anger is getting the better of you (remember, it's meant to be a tool for keeping us safe and motivating us to right wrongs) try the following:

- Whenever you feel angry, give your anger a rating out of ten so you can become aware of its intensity in different situations. Then, make a habit of stopping when it gets to a 5 or 6. Take a deep breath and ask yourself:

  * *Is it possible this event was not caused by someone trying to do me harm? Is it possible some other factor is at play?*

  * *What are 3 other possible explanations for this event?* Sometimes this is tricky in the heat of the moment, but, if you can, write them down.

  * *If I was having a really good day, would this event affect me the way it does now?* Transgressions that are worthy of anger should make us angry whether we are having a bad day or not. If you can assume that on a good day this situation would not be upsetting, then your anger has more to do with you than the situation itself.

- Go back to your Wellbeing Wheel and do the Wellbeing Audit exercise from Chapter 2 again. Focus your energy on 3 things you can do to improve your scores in the coming week. Then the following week, repeat this process.

While problematic anger and the hostile, defensive attitude that drives it can become a vicious cycle, you now know how to cultivate a healthy alternative state of being. Another vicious cycle that can be broken is that of depression. Let's explore how.

CHAPTER 9

DEPRESSION IS A VICIOUS CYCLE WAITING TO BE BROKEN

Psychological disorders are often viewed through the lens of a check-list of symptoms and diagnostic criteria. For one of the world's most common problems, depression, this all-or-nothing way of thinking promotes the notion that someone is either "depressed" or "not depressed". But what if we considered emotional functioning in terms of a continuum where at one end is major (clinical) depression and at the other is someone who has an abundance of energy, motivation, good mood, and clear thinking? We all sit somewhere on this continuum, whether diagnosed as depressed or not.

The depressed-to-thriving continuum takes into account a variety of biological, psychological, and social factors that affect our mood, sleep, energy, appetite, and libido. Working with this continuum allows us to identify low mood states and recover from them before we find ourselves facing a clinical-grade depressive episode, using principles I'll describe below. Keep in mind, clinical depression should always be tackled with the assistance of a therapist.

Even people who have never experienced depression can apply these principles and strategies to further enhance their functioning and move to the healthier end of the continuum. Let's take a look at some of them, then we'll go through some real-life examples.

The power of inertia

Of the many people I have helped recover from depression, the most consistent observation I've made that doesn't appear in any diagnostic manual is the powerful role of *inertia*. The Merriam-Webster dictionary defines inertia as "a property of matter by which it remains at rest or in uniform motion in the same straight line unless acted upon by some external force". From a psychological point of view, inertia relates to the momentum of life when we are functioning well: active, engaged, and satisfied; and the sense of 'stuck-ness' when we are not. Probably the single greatest challenge to someone recovering from depression is to summon the energy and effort to get moving again, to increase their activity levels when their every instinct is to withdraw, sleep, or shut down.

The challenge is that it takes more energy for a depressed than a non-depressed person to overcome the inertia of being stuck in a low mood state. When our energy is in low supply is precisely when we need more of it. Where a phone call here, a trip to the gym there is easy enough for someone whose energy level is high, these straightforward tasks can seem like an insurmountable obstacle to someone who's depressed.

Low mood is a vicious cycle

We know that all emotions come with a reaction urge: the adaptive effects of our primal emotional brain. The reaction urge of sadness is to withdraw. This conferred a survival advantage throughout human evolution because the helplessness, low energy, and impaired concentration associated with deep sadness rendered us more vulnerable to the dangerous outside world. The urge to withdraw was a safety-seeking mechanism that would hold us in the protective surrounds of our clan or tribe.

But the modern world is much safer than the one in which the emotional brain emerged. The short-term benefits of being withdrawn are outweighed by the longer-term costs. What happens to our mood if we stay in our room all day, don't see our friends, and don't do the things we normally do? Eventually, it's depressing.

Because withdrawal is both a cause *and* effect of depression, it creates a vicious cycle. Anyone who's experienced clinical-grade depression will tell you that cycle can be damn hard to find your way out of. In a healthy state, we might experience low mood as part of our normal life and it would not lead to entering a vicious cycle.

Sadness is a normal and healthy response to disappointment and loss. Like fear and anger, we don't want to get rid of these emotions. We just don't want to become stuck in them. When in a healthy state, our emotions should be like the weather in that we do not remain stuck in one emotion day after day. We should have the regular experience of feeling good, but we also know it is not normal to feel happy 24/7. It is normal to experience mild to moderate negative emotions as part of an active, goal-directed life, but we would expect them to come and go. It becomes a problem if we get *stuck.*

When feeling low, increase your activity levels

Remember the role of inertia in depression: it is much easier to pick up speed than get moving from a standing start, which is why prevention and early intervention are such an important focus. Noticing early signs of withdrawal or becoming stuck in low mood and then increasing activity levels is pivotal to staying out of the vicious cycle of depression. Being active, engaged, and involved in the outside world is the opposite of withdrawal. For those already stuck in a state of depressed mood, the idea of engaging with the outside world can feel like sitting at the base of a mountain and being asked to climb it. Whether trying to break the cycle or prevent it from taking hold, we need to do the very *opposite* of what our emotional brain is telling us to do. But how can we get moving when even the little things seem so hard?

Start small

The lower our mood, the lower our energy. Therefore, the lower our mood the smaller our goal should be. In the therapy room with all the support and attention of the therapist, people are prone to setting their short-term goals too high. Back in the familiar patterns of their everyday life, it can simply be too hard to follow through on what felt so achievable only days before.

Any goal set when we're at a low ebb should pass the "easy" test. That is, it should conjure the reaction of saying (or thinking) "that's easy!" Resist the temptation to raise your goal. It is more important to have the repeated experience of succeeding at a daily target, say, engaging in a moderate amount of exercise, than striving to meet bigger, seemingly more impactful goals and only occasionally achieving them. Because meeting a goal (no matter how small) is psychologically rewarding, it creates a momentum of success and the expectation to succeed, which translates into—you guessed it—more motivation and energy.

Understanding motivation

We can all relate to not being motivated to do a task: the clothes need washing, the squeaky gate needs fixing, that assignment for school needs writing, but we have no intrinsic desire to do them. And a lack of motivation is especially challenging when we're also faced with a low mood state. Unlike going into the kitchen cupboard and eating our favourite chocolate, chores such as these don't provide us with immediate reward because they are not inherently pleasurable. The satisfaction that comes from completing the job, however, comes *during* and *after* we have expended the effort. It's rewarding because the satisfaction of completing the task is pleasurable. This is the great paradox that confounds people who wait for motivation: motivation for challenging, effortful tasks comes as a result of doing them.

My mother's advice to me in childhood still rings true: starting is the hardest part and then it quickly gets much easier. When my horrifically messy bedroom began to resemble some kind of habitable environment, I started to enjoy the feeling of progress and accomplishment, and I felt more energy and commitment to the task of tidying up.

When you find yourself unable to begin a task, break it down into a series of small goals. Cleaning my messy room was a large task that overwhelmed me as a boy. But by breaking it into small tasks (like take the dirty clothes into the laundry, put the books on their shelf) it became a series of manageable tasks that I could face one at a time. Once the first small task was completed, I had the energy and motivation to take on the next small task. And soon I was seeing progress all around me. Those signs of progress motivated me to keep going.

It is important not to diminish the severity of what depression can feel like. Recovering from a depressive episode is most certainly not the same thing as cleaning your room. But the general principles of motivation hold true whether in the context of depression or not. It helps to think of motivation in this general way, so we can apply it at all stages of the continuum.

Create a cycle of activation

Feelings influence behaviour, but behaviours also influence feelings. This is especially true in the case of mood. Low mood causes withdrawal, and withdrawal causes and exacerbates low mood. Now let's look at the positive opposite of this phenomenon as it would operate further up the continuum: good mood causes the energy and desire to engage in activity, and being active causes good mood. Herein lies the secret to creating a cycle of activation.

The momentum that helps us bounce back from feeling stuck in low mood occurs in four ways:

- The reinforcement (reward) of taking action increases the likelihood we will take further action

- Our energy levels increase as a result of doing more (much like exercise increases fitness)

- Being active in various ways (exercise, social contact, exposure to sunlight) has neurochemical effects on dopamine, endorphins, oxytocin, and serotonin.

- Increased mood makes us more hopeful, engaged, and energised

Consistency is more important than magnitude. By its very nature inertia requires a sustained push of consistent action before you can be carried along by the momentum of your improved mood, energy levels, and engagement with the world around you. It is better to do something small every day or every second day, than have one big success and fall into a hole for the rest of the week.

Planning and scheduling increase success

Low mood dulls spontaneity, so decision-making during episodes of low mood tends to be more driven by feelings than logic. Using a calendar to schedule in activities in advance is a great way of ensuring you follow through. If something is planned, then there is no decision to be made, simply act on what has already been decided.

This is where our old friend psychological muscle comes into play. Psychological muscle gives us the ability to follow through and exercise self-control in the face of strong reaction urges. Just as we discovered in Chapter 6, the ability to override urges is the crucial component to taking helpful action. Psychological muscle allows us to follow through and do the pleasurable, healthy activities we schedule in even though we feel the urge to withdraw and remain inactive.

Having developed your psychological muscle with the exercises in Chapter 6, you can apply it here. Knowing you can overcome withdrawal by increasing your activity levels, schedule and then do an activity every day for the coming week. Because you know to start small and consistently accomplish small goals, make sure each activity passes the easy test. Choose from the following strategies.

Exercise

The simplest and most reliable strategy for bouncing back from a low mood state is to exercise. Vigorous exercise provides the four main functions for building positive momentum listed above, and involves a strong endorphin release. For the vast majority of people, exercise is associated with an increase in mood.

If you do not currently exercise, this could be a golden key to more energy, motivation and good feelings. Your exercise plan should pass the easy test, and ideally would be accessible regardless of external conditions (weather, the gym's open hours) that might get in the way of following through.

Please note that simple and reliable does not equate to effortless. Even though your exercise schedule passes the easy test it can still be difficult to follow through. To increase your chances of success, identify your decision point (the moment in the day when you are likely to make the decision to exercise or not), and prepare yourself in advance. Are you likely to spend the morning pondering if or when you might exercise? Instead, pair your exercise routine with daily routines you already do, such as getting out of bed in the morning (when I choose to do my exercise), or immediately after coming home from work.

Visualising yourself putting on your running shoes and walking out the door (if that's your chosen strategy) is likely to increase your chances of success. Imagining the feeling of accomplishment or improved mood after you complete the task will help too, but it is also important to identify the potential barriers to following through in advance (forgot my running shoes, I haven't done the shopping so I don't have time, it's raining), and deciding how you will overcome those barriers.

If you have selected an exercise routine that passes the easy test, is paired with a daily routine you already do, and you've identified any potential barriers in advance, the next step is to make it non-negotiable. Even when we try to identify barriers to following through, we can still get interrupted by the unexpected (I get asked to do overtime at the end of my shift, or my mother-in-law calls to ask me to fix her internet). If we assume that overcoming low mood is as important to you as helping your mother-in-law, decide that your exercise routine will be your number one priority this week, *no matter what*. This takes away the pressure to decide in the moment when an unexpected distraction comes up: the default answer will be "no".

When my client Chris was referred to me for help with symptoms of depression, I noticed that much of his Wellbeing Wheel looked good. While he described lethargy, some sleep difficulties and feeling flat; Chris also had good social supports, a meaningful job he liked and a healthy marriage. But still Chris was stuck in a rut. His life had become too routine, and he didn't exercise. When I questioned him, I realised that

Chris was prone to putting others first. He said he wanted to exercise but other things always seemed to get in the way. By finding a new challenge that involved exercise (group weight training at the local gym), and deciding that the benefits for his mood would also benefit those around him, Chris was able to make it an obligatory part of his weekly schedule. He noticed his mood and energy levels gradually return to normal over the following few weeks. Although he admitted that initially the physical effort and making exercise a priority were tough, soon it became easy and he looked forward to his gym sessions.

Social contact

Engaging with others is a powerful mood booster. Social contact can also provide support, because you suddenly don't feel alone. Furthermore, positive social interactions remind you of the pleasure that is to be had if you interact with those you care about. By planning regular social outings over a 2-3 week period, you'll find it is possible to stave off depressed moods.

This is exactly what happened with the case of Debbie. She moved to another city with her long-term partner Samuel and their three-year-old daughter when his employer asked him to set up a new office. Twelve months after the move, Samuel and Debbie's relationship broke down. Although she was able to come to terms with the end of the relationship (she said they had been having trouble for quite a while), she was feeling socially isolated, lonely, and down. After identifying the need to boost her social activity and supports, Debbie joined a local mothers' group, attended a fundraising event for her daughter's kindergarten, and hosted an afternoon tea for the small number of people she did know and like in her local area. Although doing these things took some effort and did not instantly change her life, Debbie found she regained her energy and motivation to reach out to others. Taking those initial steps set her on the path to building a new social circle of friends and other supportive connections.

In addition to increasing activity levels by way of exercise or social contact, there are a few mini-strategies and tips that can help prevent or reduce low mood:

Sunlight

Morning sunlight is a great way to boost your serotonin levels naturally. A morning walk in the sun is a great way to lift your mood and brighten your outlook for the day. Regular sunlight exposure helps maintain healthy serotonin levels, which in turn plays a major role in how you feel. For people who are particularly affected by seasonal changes and get the winter blues (more formally known as Seasonal Affective Disorder), sunlight exposure is an important remedy and prevention strategy.

Cold exposure

Finishing your shower under cold water could boost your mood and mental clarity to start your day. Although there is a lack of research into the specific mechanisms by which mood can be improved through cold exposure, it is thought to increase noradrenaline, which is important for the chemical balance of the brain. There is also an abundance of anecdotal evidence that for some people a dose of cold water gives them a real boost in alertness and overall sense of wellbeing.

For me, cold exposure involves walking my dog in the middle of winter wearing only a t-shirt and shorts. Not only does this energise me for the day, it gives me a sense of mental toughness to willingly step into discomfort like that. Over time I have built up an amazing tolerance for the cold. Shivering friends repeatedly offer me jackets only for me to realise I'm the only person not wearing one.

Plan for variety

When you're feeling low and have less mental energy than usual, you'll be much more likely to live by habit. This includes mundane choices like what to eat, what to wear, and where to go. New or different experiences are more likely to provide pleasure and stimulation than simply doing the same thing every day. Try having something different for lunch, like a sandwich filling or salad bowl you've never tried before. Or wear a jacket to work that you haven't worn in a while. These little varieties all help add momentum to your cycle of activation.

To Do and Digest

Moving up the depression to thriving continuum is about taking helpful action. Actions to increase your activity levels can include exercise and social engagements. Mini-strategies include sunlight, cold exposure, and increasing variety in small ways. When implemented consistently, each of these helps build momentum, increase energy, and improve mood.

Ultimately, taking action will change our mindset. Just as exposure to what we fear changes our beliefs about fear, danger, and our ability to face the world around us, becoming active and engaged during periods of persistent low mood begins to positively shape our thoughts and beliefs about ourselves, our relationships, and our future.

Thinking is implicated in all the major issues we have discussed so far, and can be used as a powerful psychological asset to help us attain greater wellbeing. But the key to unlocking the power of your thinking can only come from first understanding how thoughts work.

CHAPTER 10

THOUGHTS AFFECT HOW YOU FEEL BUT ARE OFTEN INACCURATE

OFTEN WHEN I meet new people and the word "psychologist" comes up, they will self-consciously joke that I might be "analysing" them. This reaction reveals a common assumption about the nature of modern psychology: that there is a deep, hidden, almost esoteric meaning behind what people say and do.

Although we *are* influenced by subconscious psychological factors, they are actually just natural and understandable characteristics that make sense when considered in the context of our life experiences. Most commonly, these subconscious influences are our thoughts and beliefs. Rather than something mystical, sub-conscious simply means *beneath our conscious awareness*.

Many of the things we think and believe operate outside of our conscious awareness, yet they hold a very strong influence on both feelings and behaviour. In fact, so much of our day-to-day thinking occurs on autopilot, that psychologists refer to it as automatic thinking.

How automatic thinking works

Imagine how difficult it would be to get through the day if we had to be consciously aware of every single thought, every minor intention to open a door or pick up a pen, or every step in daily routines like making a cup of tea. These tasks would be mentally laborious and we'd be exhausted by lunchtime. Automatic thinking saves us time and energy.

But there is a downside to automatic thinking. It can lead us to emotional states that do not befit the situation at hand.

Consider this: You've arranged to meet a friend at a café, and half an hour has passed since the agreed meeting time, yet your friend has not arrived. What kind of feelings might you have in this situation?

Take a moment to pause and consider what your instinctive emotional reaction might be. You may feel:

- annoyed or even angry,
- worried or anxious,
- down or dejected, or
- calm, without much of an emotional reaction at all.

Of course, the context of the situation will influence the emotional outcome here. Is the friend usually late? Has this happened to you before? Are there any extenuating circumstances like traffic or weather conditions?

For each possible emotional response, the event is the same. The friend hasn't arrived and we don't know why. It is in this quiet space, perhaps dozens of little daily ambiguities, that our subconscious mind leaves its imprint like footsteps in the snow.

Without a lens into their subconscious, most people experience this scenario as the event causing them to have an emotional reaction:

EVENT → FEELING

Psychologists have learnt, however, that that is not really what's happening here. There is an important middle step that occurs outside of conscious awareness that is actually what causes the emotion: your automatic thoughts.

EVENT → AUTOMATIC THOUGHTS → FEELING

Take a look at the following examples:

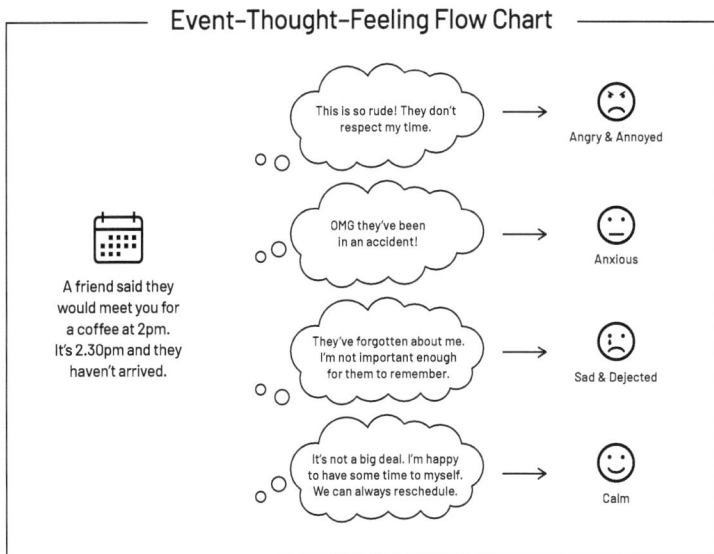

Event-Thought-Feeling Flow Chart

A friend said they would meet you for a coffee at 2pm. It's 2.30pm and they haven't arrived.

This is so rude! They don't respect my time. → Angry & Annoyed

OMG they've been in an accident! → Anxious

They've forgotten about me. I'm not important enough for them to remember. → Sad & Dejected

It's not a big deal. I'm happy to have some time to myself. We can always reschedule. → Calm

Each feeling would fit the imagined scenario if the respective automatic thought were true. But without knowing why the friend is late, we can see that the feeling is being caused by the automatic thought and not the event of waiting for a friend who is late.

The various emotions that someone might experience are quite different, yet in each instance the event that causes them—waiting for a friend who is late—is *exactly the same*. This demonstrates that it is not the event that causes the feeling, it is the thoughts or interpretation that cause the feeling.

Becoming aware of automatic thoughts

Usually, we aren't consciously aware of our automatic thoughts, just our feelings. But if someone asks us "why are you feeling this way?", we could start to delve into the content of the automatic thoughts. By keeping a diary or journal of the moments when we are affected by strong emotion, we can uncover the thinking behind the feelings. Thinking is often represented in words, as in what we "say" to ourselves in our head (our self-talk), but it can also be imagery, like a scene or a movie in our mind's eye. Those scenes can be described in words to help us become aware of our automatic thoughts and how they affect us.

A very simple prompt to help you become aware of automatic thoughts is to write down the following sentence every time you have a strong emotional reaction to something:

When _____ *I was feeling* _____ *because I was thinking* _____.

The structure of these sentences differs from the way we examined the scenario of the late friend in the figure above. There, we looked at the causal process of:

EVENT → AUTOMATIC THOUGHTS → FEELING

Here, the sentence structure asks you to identify the emotion first. This is because it is much easier to identify the feelings than the automatic thought. Noticing strong feelings first and then filling in these gaps prompts us to identify the thoughts that caused our emotions. It helps us put these automatic thoughts into words on the page in front of us.

For example:

When *I went into the job interview,* I was feeling *panicked,* because I was thinking *I'm going to completely bomb out.*

Or,

When *my boyfriend left to go on his business trip,* I was feeling *insecure and anxious* because I was thinking *about all the opportunities he would have to cheat on me.*

Or,

When *my sister's boyfriend jokingly teased me about the tie I was wearing at a wedding,* I was feeling *anger and hurt* because I was thinking *about the memory of being teased at school by kids who always made fun of how I looked.*

Or,

When *I was about to open the meeting I had been asked to chair,* I was feeling *anxious and stressed* because I was thinking *my colleagues will be argumentative and defiant.*

With practice, it becomes easier to identify our automatic thoughts and bring this unconscious process more easily into the realm of self-awareness.

Our thoughts are often wrong

Most of our brain's automatic processes are designed for speed and efficiency. The down-side of this mental corner-cutting is that automatic thoughts can be, and often are, inaccurate; or at the very least do not give us the whole picture. Not all of the interpretations in response to the absent friend can be true.

Thankfully, many of the problematic mental shortcuts our brains can take can be readily identified. These shortcuts are sometimes called Thinking Errors. Common Thinking Errors include:

Black-or-White Thinking

Black-or-white thinking is the tendency to think in terms of "all" or "nothing" rather than appreciate the shades of grey that tend to more accurately reflect the world around us. For example, "If I don't get the promotion, I will have failed." This does not factor in the reality that missing out on a promotion is not a complete failure, it is an obstacle or delay toward an important goal.

Discounting the positive and magnifying the negative

Discounting the positive and magnifying the negative is the tendency to automatically dismiss or devalue something good that happens, or to focus instead on a relatively minor occurrence that distracts from the good thing. For example, if someone compliments us and we say to ourselves "they're just trying to be nice," we discard an opportunity to feel good and automatically insert a negative self-depreciating thought that makes us feel worse.

Shoulds (should / must / always / never)

When you notice the use of words like "should", "must", "always" or "never" it is an indication of rigid, rule-based thinking. For example, "I must always say yes when someone asks for my help" creates a rule that is likely at some point to cause problems. A more flexible approach would be, "It is good to help others when I can, but it is OK to say no." Flexible thoughts and beliefs give rise to flexibility and adaptability in behaviour, a healthy and helpful characteristic that is worth striving for.

Overgeneralising

Overgeneralising occurs when we draw broad conclusions from one instance of behaviour or one piece of evidence. If we lose our cool in a family argument and conclude "I am a terrible parent", we are assessing our entire character based on one instance only. Overgeneralising doesn't appreciate the fact that our behaviour and performance will vary according to the day, context, and many other factors.

Labelling

Like overgeneralisation, labelling ascribes permanent, sweeping assessments that usually are not justified from one event alone. To call yourself an idiot because you spill your coffee on the desk is a harsh self-judgement that does not consider all the non-idiotic things you do and have done. It is rare that a broad label accurately or fairly captures all there is to a person, and is therefore either incomplete or erroneous.

Fortune telling

So often we play fictional movies in our mind of what we think is going to happen next, when in reality we cannot know how something is going to turn out. But, like real-life movies, these thoughts can take us for an emotional ride. We might visualise tomorrow's meeting ending in humiliation, or think "tomorrow's meeting is going to be a disaster", but our ability to accurately predict the future in detail is generally poor.

Mind reading

Like fortune telling, mind reading is another supernatural ability our automatic brains assume to have acquired. As absurd as it sounds, the belief that we know another person's mind is surprisingly common. A conclusion such as "that person doesn't like me", if based on scant evidence, will often turn out to be inaccurate.

Catastrophising

Catastrophising is a hallmark of anxiety, a dramatic over-estimation of risk to the point of blowing things out of all proportion. This is the thinking error that causes someone to assume that because their friend is five minutes late, they must have been killed in a car accident.

Emotional reasoning

Emotional reasoning is the inference that because we feel something, it must be true. If we *feel* embarrassed, it must mean we've said or done something stupid. If we *feel* self-conscious, it must mean everyone is looking at us. If we *feel* angry, it must mean someone has transgressed against us.

Personalisation

Personalizing is when we attribute an event to ourselves when it does not relate directly to us. For example, if your partner thinks you're mad at them when you're just being quiet or reflective. We saw how this operates in causing anger in Chapter 8. Personalisation can result in feeling overwhelmed, guilty, angry, or anxious.

As you become more aware of your automatic thoughts, look out for these thinking errors in your self-talk. You will also begin to notice these thinking errors being made by others through what they say.

Thinking errors, by definition, lead us to emotional outcomes that don't properly reflect the situation at hand. There's no harm in experiencing any emotion if it is befitting the situation and especially if we make good decisions in response to it. Inaccurate thinking leads to ill-fitting emotions and emotional reaction urges, and predisposes unhelpful decision-making. As Aristotle said of anger:

> *"Anybody can become angry - that is easy, but to be angry with the right person and to the right degree and at the right time and for the right purpose and in the right way - that is not within everybody's power and is not easy."*

The challenge then, is to start with "right" thinking, which leads us to experience the "right" emotions. While we are all prone to thinking errors from time to time, particularly when we are under stress, persistent, repetitive habits of thinking can cause serious problems.

Unhelpful habits of thinking

The example of a friend who is late to meet you for coffee seems insignificant, and for many people, a single automatic thought doesn't reveal any negative patterns in their underlying psychology. But what if *most* of your life events generated an angry automatic thought, or an anxious one, or a depressive one? Your friend doesn't return your email? They might be rude and inconsiderate. Or stabbed in the heart by an intruder. Or you're not worth replying to anyway, why would anyone bother? Having a bias toward one way of thinking creates a habit of interpreting life events, a lens that colours your perception of any ambiguity that arises.

Do and Digest

Here's how to tell if you have an unhelpful habit of thinking. In journaling your automatic thoughts, do you notice:

- Angry thinking that *consistently* over-estimates hostile intent?

- Anxious thinking that *consistently* over-estimates the likelihood of things going wrong, and how bad it would be if something did go wrong?

- Depressive thinking that is *consistently* overly negative about yourself, the world, or the future?

If you do, you are predisposing yourself to becoming stuck in a state of anger, anxiety or depression. Your emotions are less likely to flow naturally like the weather, and the quality of your decision-making and enjoyment of life is likely to suffer.

Whether through thinking errors or unhelpful habits of thinking, chances are you are sensing some of your own subconscious habits of thought rising to the conscious surface of your mind. You may have just identified several pitfalls that until now were blissfully submerged. And I didn't need esoteric powers. I didn't need to "analyse" you. I simply drew your attention to a process that was previously beneath your normal awareness. More importantly: what are we going to do about it?

If thoughts cause feelings, it follows that balanced thinking leads to a more balanced emotional life. Identifying these thinking errors and habits in yourself and others will give rise to seeing *alternatives* and therefore the possibility of a more nuanced, accurate, and balanced view of yourself and the events in your life.

Alternatives provide freedom of thought. They are the foundation for developing one of the most powerful psychological tools of all. A tool which, if you can master it to the point of internalising its principles, will break the cycle of unhelpful patterns and choices and allow you to face life on a level playing field...no, a playing field that is tipped in your favour!

You are now ready to learn The Helpful Thinking Process.

CHAPTER UPGRADE

Get your Thinking Error Summary Sheet at:

www.tomnehmy.com/applesupgrades

CHAPTER 11

LEARN AND LIVE THE HELPFUL THINKING PROCESS

It had been days and I was still seething.

A disagreement with a work colleague was still replaying over and over in my head, and I was stuck in anger. The colleague had been arrogant and rude and not the least bit collegial, and what's more I had since been proven right in the dispute over an important and time-consuming project. The fact that I had this hot anger sitting in my gut nearly a week later meant I had shifted from my usual healthy state, with my emotions like the weather, to being *stuck* in negative emotion. Now it was a problem. Almost all definitions for when an emotional reaction becomes a problem include a criterion of duration, such as an emotional state that has endured for several days or weeks without change.

I needed to work through this for two reasons:

First, so I could *make a good decision* about what to do (or *not* do, as the case may be) in response to it.

Second, so I could *let it go*. I wanted to return to the usual ebb and flow of a healthy daily emotional life and focus on my wellbeing.

As you may have experienced, anger is a powerfully motivating feeling and the reaction urge of lashing out can be hard to resist. But it can also be irrational and ill-advised. I fantasised about confronting the colleague, and thought about all the cutting and damning things I wanted to say. But before I was to take such drastic action, I really needed to know for my own sake and the sake of my career, if it would be the most helpful option. Thankfully, in the midst of this powerful emotional state, the Helpful Thinking Process guided me to decide against it and move forward.

The Helpful Thinking Process

We have learnt that it's not the events of our lives that cause our feelings, it's our thoughts or interpretations of events, and these are often subconscious and automatic. They also often contain thinking errors or habitual biases that mean our emotions and subsequent reaction urges may not appropriately reflect the situation at hand. They might also predispose us to respond in an unhelpful way.

This presents a golden opportunity: to learn a type of balanced thinking that will lead to a more balanced emotional life and better decisions in response to life's events.

The Helpful Thinking Process is a step-by-step writing task that guides us through a series of specific questions. It aims to challenge and test our automatic thoughts to ensure they meet the criteria for the ideal mode of thinking. This ideal mode of thinking is:

1. **Balanced**. Balanced thinking compels us to explore alternatives.

2. **Realistic**. Realistic thinking compels us to explore likelihood.

3. **Helpful**. Helpful thinking compels us to explore our purpose.

When to use it

We should use the Helpful Thinking Process whenever we are concerned about our emotions' intensity, type or duration.

- *Intensity.* If we are concerned that the emotion we're experiencing might not fit the situation, because it might be an over-reaction or under-reaction to whatever's happened, the Helpful Thinking Process will guide us toward a thought that generates an emotion that is appropriate in its strength.

- *Type.* If something that would normally be a happy occasion feels sad, and we aren't quite sure why, the Helpful Thinking Process can assist us to figure it out.

- *Duration.* If we are feeling stuck in a state of negative emotion, our emotions are not like the weather. If we are experiencing a negative emotion that dominates our mood for several days in a row, chances are we're at risk of becoming stuck. The Helpful Thinking Process can help us make good decisions that allow us to move through the emotion and back into balance.

In the example above, I knew it was time for me to check my thinking, because my emotions were most definitely not like the weather. I had felt angry for days on end. What's more, the intensity of what I was feeling was very high. I wasn't just annoyed, I was *furious*! In this instance, both the duration and intensity of what I was feeling were cause for checking my thinking.

A structured writing task *is* a structured thinking task

If you are prompted to write something down, you must *think* it first. The act of writing in a structured fashion, as we are about to detail here, will immediately get us off automatic pilot so we can consider alternative information, possibilities, and perspectives. At the end of the process we will have thoroughly explored all the available information and can therefore come to the most appropriate perspective. Rather than being defined by thinking errors or biases that come about from our habits of thinking, the conclusion we draw will be well informed, fresh from the skewed way we might view the world, and free from the sometimes oppressive rule of the emotional brain.

Practising the Helpful Thinking Process can not only serve you well in times that you get stuck in a negative emotion, it can also train your brain to think in flexible ways. By routinely filling out the template (writing by hand or typing it out) you are building and strengthening the neural pathways that support complex thought.

The process

Here's how the Helpful Thinking Process works. Take a look at the steps in table form below, then we'll look at the steps in more detail, and finally we'll use the process to work through an example.

Step 1. What is my automatic thought?	Write it down:	What is the feeling?
		How strong is it out of 10?
Step 2. What are three other possible outcomes or explanations?	Write them down:	
Step 3. What has happened in the past in this situation, and what is most likely to happen now?	Write it down:	
Step 4. What would my thinking brain say, compared to my emotional brain?	Write it down:	
Step 5. How would I advise a friend in this situation?	Write it down:	

Step 6. Given what I've written above, how could I re-write my original thought (from Step 1), to make it more: ✓ Balanced ✓ Realistic ✓ Helpful?	Write your more balanced, realistic, and helpful thought here:	What is your feeling now? How strong is your feeling now, out of 10?
Step 7. My helpful course of action is:		

[To download a copy of the template, see the Chapter Upgrade at the end of the chapter, or simply visit *www.tomnehmy.com/applesupgrades*]

Step 1. Your automatic thought(s): making the subconscious conscious. *What am I thinking? What is my automatic thought?* Automatic thoughts are the phrases or statements we make in the back of our minds, without being consciously aware of it. We can learn to become aware of our automatic thoughts by stopping and tuning in to the interpretation or prediction we've made that is driving the current emotion.

Next, write down the feeling that comes from that thought. Is it anxiety? Anger? Sadness? Then write how strong the feeling is out of ten, where ten would be the strongest possible level of that emotion.

Step 2. Flexible thinking: getting off autopilot and finding balance through alternatives. *What are three other possible* outcomes, explanations, or pieces of evidence I haven't yet considered?

This step is about going beyond the automatic processing and consciously incorporating different perspectives that we would never consider on automatic pilot. Take a moment to explore alternatives. Even if you are not sure you believe the alternatives, it is very important to explore them. It's fine to treat it as an intellectual exercise; we can evaluate the likelihood of these alternatives later. For now, come up with several bits of information pertaining to this situation that you missed. It may even help to explore the point of view of any other person involved in this situation, or to play the role of a devil's advocate and look for opposing arguments or evidence that does not support your automatic thought. By considering several alternative viewpoints and shades of grey, we are ensuring that we are being balanced and not one-sided. Write them down.

This is also a good step to identify if we are making any of the thinking errors detailed in Chapter 10. If we notice a thinking error, it will prompt us for an alternative point of view to explore. For example, if we notice we are overgeneralising, that observation can help us find a perspective that is more specific and accurate.

Step 3. Realistic thinking: evaluating likelihood. *What has happened in the past in this situation, and what is most likely to happen now?*

Here, we are starting to tap into realistic thinking. Unhelpful thinking biases tend to over- or under-estimate the likelihood of certain conclusions being true. We can also ask, what has happened to others in this situation in the past? On average, what is the most common outcome? Write it down.

Step 4. Engaging the thinking brain: searching for evidence and logic. *What would my thinking brain say compared to my emotional brain?*

This step appeals to logic and objective facts. When viewed through the lens of strong emotion, our attention and perceptions can be greatly coloured by those feelings. This step implores us to try to look at the situation in a scientist-in-a-lab-coat kind of way. Write this perspective down.

Step 5. Helpful thinking through an arm's length perspective. *How would I advise a friend in this situation?*

It's often easier to be a wise sage to those around us than to apply wisdom to our own conundrums. But it's possible to get closer to those genuine wise words if we imagine that exact scenario. Set the scene in your mind and imagine this was happening to a friend. From this arm's length perspective, what would you say to your friend that would be helpful? Write it down.

Step 6. Integration and summary. *Given what I've written in the steps above, how could I re-write my original thought to make it more balanced, realistic, and helpful?*

This step is where we bring all the different perspectives, evidence, and explanations together. For the sake of validating my initial response to the situation, I write that it is possible my automatic thought is true, no matter how catastrophic. This acknowledges the reality that sometimes shit happens, and the worst-case scenario can, on rare occasion, be true. But then I will incorporate the most accurate and sensible points before coming to a conclusion. Notice that you will write more in this step than in any of the previous steps.

Start by writing down "**Sure, it's possible...**" then add the automatic thought. The following sentences should start with the word "**But,**" and include the best points from the other steps above. Be sure to include the most surprising, convincing, or powerful points you came up with. Then write "**Chances are...**" and come up with a conclusion that is the most likely outcome or explanation.

Now write down the feeling that comes from this more balanced, realistic, helpful thinking. Next write down the strength of that feeling. It may be the same general feeling but lower in strength, or the feeling itself may have changed. It is unlikely that this process will take you from the depth of despair to jumping for joy, and that isn't the intention. The intention is to get your thinking and emotions to reasonably reflect the situation at hand.

Step 7. Choose a helpful course of action. Arguably the most important step in the Helpful Thinking Process is the decision about what to do. Helpful action can salvage something good from even the most testing scenario.

Please keep in mind the Helpful Thinking Process doesn't tell you what to think. It is about giving you a tool to explore your own perspectives, evidence, and decision-making. No two people will complete the template in exactly the same way, even if they are in similar circumstances.

Helpful Thinking in action

Let's look at an example of how this works.
The Situation:

*You walk past a colleague at work and
smile. They seem to look up at you but
they keep on walking. They don't say
anything and they don't seem to smile.*

Step 1. What am I thinking? What is my automatic thought?

*'They must be annoyed with me.
What have I done?'*

[Feeling – worried, anxious 7/10]

Step 2. What are three other possible outcomes, explanations, or pieces of evidence I haven't yet considered?

1. *Maybe they didn't see me, even though it looked like they were looking at me.*

2. *Maybe they are really preoccupied with or worried about something. I know that a lot of people are stressed with deadlines around here.*

3. *My automatic thought is an example of "mind reading" (a thinking error) – I don't know for sure what they are thinking and feeling, I cannot definitively conclude they are angry. My automatic thought is also "personalising" (a thinking error), I needn't assume whatever is going on for this person is necessarily to do with me.*

Step 3. What has happened in the past in this situation? What is most likely to happen now?

Well, last time I thought someone ignored me,
last month when I was at a party, it turns out
they were just caught up in their own world.
That's a likely possibility this time as well.

Step 4. What would my thinking brain say compared to my emotional brain?

This person is my colleague and friend,
and I have no evidence to suggest
that they are angry with me.

Step 5. How would I advise a friend in this situation?

If a friend asked my advice, I would say to
them "don't jump to conclusions until you
have some evidence. Why not speak to them
and find out for sure what's going on?"

Step 6. Given what I've written in the steps above, how could I re-write my original thought to make it more balanced, realistic, and helpful?

Sure *there's a chance they're angry with me.* ***But***
it's also possible they were distracted or didn't
see me. There's no evidence or reason why they
would be angry. The last time this happened
the other person was just caught up in their
own world. ***Chances are*** *there's nothing really*
bad going on. I can talk to them later today.

[Feeling: Curious, concerned – 3/10]

Step 7. My helpful course of action is:

I will talk to them later and ask how they are.

The revised helpful thought (Step 6) follows the structure of *Sure, But, Chances are….* I like this because it acknowledges the reality that on rare occasions a catastrophic thought might be true. It also refutes a common assumption that helpful thinking is all about positive thinking. Helpful thinking is about balanced, realistic, and helpful thoughts, while positive thinking is about focusing on the most optimistic perspective no matter how narrow, fanciful, and deleterious it may be.

Importantly, the revised thought is generally much more accurate than the automatic thought. Not only does it feel better, it is more likely to be true. In terms of the resulting emotion, there is still some residual concern which is natural and appropriate. But the difference between the emotion generated by the automatic thought and the subsequent emotion generated by the helpful thought is significant and of tangible benefit.

The Helpful Thinking Process is a sophisticated tool to help us to retrain our brain to naturally think in more balanced, helpful, realistic ways. Just as a sophisticated process like driving a car becomes automatic through practice, so too can thinking skills.

The principle, without practice, is not enough

Understanding the concepts behind the process is not enough. Many of my clients will say "I get it" and then expect to be able to apply the Helpful Thinking Process in their day to day life, in times of stress and emotion, and on the fly. Often these people will believe they are using their helpful thinking skills when they are not, and they mistakenly conclude that it doesn't work. The reason why we need to sit down and write (or type) during the times we most need to use this process is that stress, strong emotions, tiredness, distractions, and habit all make it more likely that we are operating on automatic pilot. Automatic pilot, by nature, is not aware of the options. It does not remind us to stop and think and figure things out by exploring several different angles. We need to first realise that being stuck in negative emotion (or concerned enough to want to check our thinking), is a signal to sit down and complete the template. Then we can routinely practise, apply, and strengthen these sophisticated cognitive skills.

To Do and Digest

Practise the Helpful Thinking Process. Download the template and actively look for an opportunity to complete it in the coming week. Alternatively, you may be able to use an example from the recent past for the sake of practising this important skill. There may even be something on your mind right now that would benefit from helpful thinking.

Get your free copy of the Helpful Thinking Process PDF template at:

www.tomnehmy.com/applesupgrades

CHAPTER 12

THE DEBATING METHOD CREATES SUPERFAST HELPFUL THINKING

WHEN YOU GET the hang of the Helpful Thinking Process, it will feel more natural. You will easily identify many perspectives and different pieces of evidence relevant to your situation. Your brain will become more efficient. The neuronal pathways relevant to helpful thinking will become powerfully activated, and you may find yourself becoming more effective at things like brainstorming or seeing new perspectives even in different contexts. You will also naturally start to identify thinking errors in what people say. Don't be surprised if you are the one generating solutions in business meetings, or if friends and colleagues start gravitating toward you for advice.

Once you've become adept at helpful thinking, you can start using a shortcut version and still derive similar benefit. Don't skip over learning the full process and go straight to this one, however. You should use all the steps until you find you are able to very quickly and easily generate multiple options for each step of the process. Then you'll be ready for this simplified version.

How to use the Debating Method

Here's how it works: grab a blank piece of paper and draw a line straight down the middle (or if you are always in front of a computer, open a blank document and create a table with two columns). On the top left, write out your negative automatic thought(s). As you know by now, these will be brief, often black-or-white statements or conclusions, possibly with a catastrophic, self-defeating, or hostile flavour that often accompanies strong negative emotions. On the right side, write down a truthful statement that acknowledges the possibility that the negative automatic thought might be true (remember, shit happens). Then, still in the right column, imagine you were on a debating team and had been allocated the task of arguing against the automatic thought(s). Come up with as many good arguments as you can that challenge them. We want to retain the Sure, But, Chances are... structure from the final step of the full Helpful Thinking Process.

Now, let's take a look at an example:

The Event or Situation: Peter's wife has just told him his mother-in-law is coming for dinner. It will be the first family dinner she's attended in nearly 12 months, after he banned her for meddling, bossing, and criticising.

Negative automatic thought(s)	Balanced, Realistic, Helpful thinking
This will be a disaster. She can never keep her nose out of our business. She's a troll.	

Peter's negative automatic thoughts are catastrophic (even if understandable), and probably generate a strong feeling of resentment, annoyance, and anxiety too. If just left with his negative automatic thoughts, he will not only be left with these feelings for as long as he ruminates about the dinner, he will also engage in unhelpful reaction behaviours such as making snide comments, avoiding the dining room until the very last minute, or displaying body language that invokes a defensive atmosphere.

Note that in this situation, Peter is also more vulnerable to a hostile attribution bias (assuming hostile intent on the part of his mother-in-law, see Chapter 8). This could result in an ambiguous scenario being interpreted as an act of hostility. For example, if his mother-in-law does not give him a kiss when she first sees him, it may well be a result of her feeling nervous or unwelcome. Peter, however, might assume it is an intentionally dismissive act toward him.

Given the history to this situation and the stakes being quite high (it's still his wife's mother, after all), it's very important that Peter challenge his automatic thinking. He's identified his automatic thoughts and recognises the need to challenge them, but just as he decides to put his helpful thinking skills to good use, he hears her car pulling into the driveway. What does he need to do to generate helpful thinking in record time?

Remember school debating contests? You would be allocated a side to argue for, regardless of whether you personally believed it or not. The quality of the argument was more important than the level of belief. To this end, it is important that we try to come up with arguments or statements that can reasonably be considered to be true.

Remember, the goal is not positive thinking, optimism, winning, or even being happy (good mood). The goal is to cultivate *realistic*, *balanced*, and *helpful* thinking, and to make helpful decisions about what to *do*.

In the case of Peter, he starts the process feeling annoyed, perhaps angry, and certainly pessimistic about the dinner ahead. If he follows the Debating Method, he might come up with the following:

First, he acknowledges that his automatic thought(s) might be true:

Negative automatic thought(s)	Balanced, Realistic, Helpful thinking
This will be a disaster. *She can never keep her nose out of our business.* *She's a troll.*	**Sure**, it *might* be a disaster.

Then, like the debater, Peter needs to come up with true statements that challenge the automatic thoughts. Because these thoughts don't come as naturally as his habitual or automatic responses in the left column, it might seem difficult. But if he stops and thinks about it for a few moments (controlled processing) he will be able to come up with some useful points, which go under the word "But" in the column on the right:

Negative automatic thought(s)	Balanced, Realistic, Helpful thinking
This will be a disaster. *She can never keep her nose out of our business.* *She's a troll.*	**Sure**, it *might* be a disaster. **But:** - Deep down she does actually want the best for us, even if she goes about it the wrong way. - While I do find her annoying overall, she does have some good qualities. - My wife would appreciate us mending the relationship. I can focus on the benefits to my wife and our marriage. - If I put in extra effort tonight, the dinner might turn out differently to the way it has in the past. I can't control her, but I can control my reactions. - My mother-in-law might have a different attitude tonight after the time apart.

Finally, he needs to come up with a summary statement. This may not be as detailed as in the step-by-step Helpful Thinking Process, but it should be a brief or general reflection of the major arguments for the column on the right:

Negative automatic thought(s)	Balanced, Realistic, Helpful thinking
This will be a disaster. *She can never keep her nose out of our business.* *She's a troll.*	**Sure**, it *might* be a disaster. **But:** - Deep down she does actually want the best for us, even if she goes about it the wrong way. - While I do find her annoying overall, she does have some good qualities. - My wife would appreciate us mending the relationship. I can focus on the benefits to my wife and our marriage. - If I put in extra effort tonight, the dinner might turn out differently to the way it has in the past. I can't control her, but I can control my reactions. - My mother-in-law might have a different attitude tonight after the time apart. **Chances are:** If I put in some extra effort the dinner could go ok. If I can be patient and do what I can to make it go smoothly, it will help my wife and might pave the way for a better relationship.

The Sure, But, Chances are… structure is a simple yet compelling way to quickly engage our helpful thinking skills, without the multiple questions in the full Helpful Thinking

Process. Hopefully for Peter, the evening will turn out well. If it does go pear-shaped, he'll still be able to rely on his psychological muscle and the Magic Question ("what is the helpful thing to do now?") to respond sensibly and effectively.

To Do and Digest

Once you feel the Helpful Thinking Process from the last chapter is familiar and understood, try the Debating Method. While some people assume that knowing the principles of helpful thinking are enough to become immediately competent (it isn't), it is the people who build their competence through practising the increasingly shortened steps presented in this book who make helpful thinking a more natural, even habitual, process.

Advanced tip: When you have had practice with the Debating Method, try to do it out loud, on the go, without writing anything down. When speaking out loud to yourself, remember to be guided by the structure of Sure, But, Chances are…. If you can get to this level, congratulations! You are now a Helpful Thinking virtuoso!

CHAPTER 13

MANAGING STRESS IS ABOUT HAVING THE RIGHT AMOUNT AT THE RIGHT TIME

WHEN JOHN GRAY, author of the mega-selling book *Men Are from Mars, Women are from Venus* first conducted workshops, he was so paralysed by fear and stress that he collapsed. Because of the intense focus of the audience's gaze, the distraction of his racing heart, sweaty palms, and dry throat, all he wanted to do was flee the stage and escape to safety. Thankfully, John made a decision to resist that urge. He persisted in presenting his workshops, has built an enormously successful business, and has helped thousands of people.

If you want to succeed and achieve in life, you'll have to conquer the one hurdle we all must eventually face: acceptance of a certain amount of discomfort that comes from an active, goal-directed life.

To participate fully in life is to accept that sometimes we will find ourselves outside our comfort zone. Stress, fatigue, fear of failure, uncertainty, and even boredom are all forms of discomfort that we must endure if we are to follow through on our greatest ambitions. The effort that goes into using our psychological muscle when overriding a reaction urge is a necessary discomfort. As is following through on the Magic Question when we know the most helpful course of action is also demanding and difficult.

For those who have had a particularly easy life or who have been overprotected, handling discomfort can be an exceptionally difficult challenge. To reject discomfort in exchange for our comfort zones can manifest itself as avoidance, escape, pro-crastination, self-sabotage, reassurance-seeking, and giving-up behaviours.

The question that sits at the fork in the road whenever we face taking on a challenge is: "What is more important, to be comfortable or to reach this goal?"

Being out of your comfort zone, by definition, is stressful. Of the many myths surrounding the concept of stress, the one I encounter most often is that it is inherently harmful or bad, and something to get rid of. But this attitude ignores the reality that stress and its associated sensations and urges are actually *necessary* if we want to be at our best.

Stress is essential for optimal functioning

We all seek periods that are stress-free (think holidays, retreats) and these can be extremely beneficial as a temporary break from the usual demands and pace of life. But if we had no stress during a major project, before an exam, or when a deadline is looming, we would be likely to perform worse than someone who is experiencing some stress. The upside of stress is that it brings focus, alertness, energy, and motivation that is simply not present in a stress-free state.

Although little or no stress is associated with pleasant sensations of calm, relaxation, and peacefulness, how many important goals in the real world can be best accomplished in that state? The urge to tackle your end of semester paper is totally incongruent with relaxation. Being driven to deliver the most energetic sales pitch in the make-or-break business meeting is simply incompatible with feeling perfectly calm. And if my football team makes it to the Grand Final this year, I absolutely do not want them in a zen-like state in the locker rooms before they go out to play. I want sweaty palms and butterflies in the stomach!

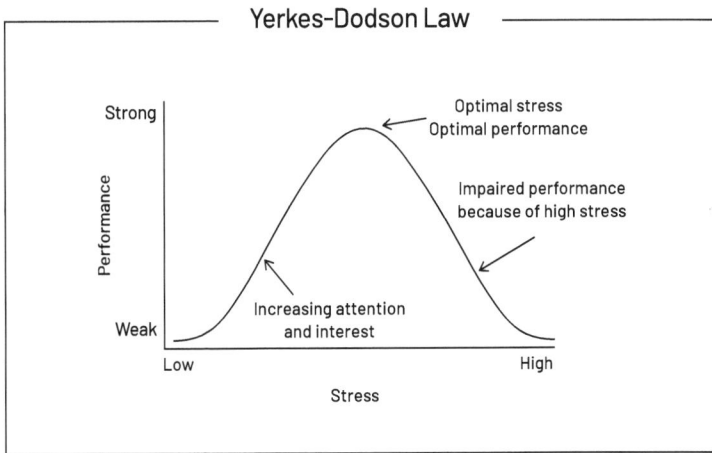

The Yerkes-Dodson Law is the principle that our performance on most tasks will increase as our stress levels increase, until the stress gets too strong, and then our performance will decrease.

Helpful stress is like the milder cousin of anxiety. Concern and pressure to perform are present and keep us focused, but panic or fear, which could impair our efforts, are not present. Much like the physiology of anxiety, both good and bad stress can bring adrenaline with particular bodily sensations like sweating, feeling hot, and increased heart rate and respiration.

To be sure, the feeling of stress can be uncomfortable, even if it is in a helpful dose. If our tightly held goal is to lead a comfortable life then we are likely to interpret the feeling of stress as something that is to be avoided. If that's our aim (the comfortable, stress-free life) then we must also accept that it will be a smaller life with fewer achievements and a softer, less enduring footprint in the world.

We should make no moral judgement of the person who chooses to pursue comfort over stress. It is a legitimate choice that does have its advantages. And for anyone who has experienced traumatic stress or serious chronic stress, it is completely understandable.

Instead, observing the different lives and lifestyles of those willing to encounter stress and those who simply want the comfortable life, allows us to make an informed decision about our own relationship to stress. For the comfortable life is not the impactful life. Bold explorers, trailblazers, and risk-takers find a way to exist comfortably in a state of discomfort. They recognise and welcome stress as a tool that is part and parcel of the journey toward their significant and demanding goals.

Knowing that the uncomfortable, enlivening state of moderate stress is not harmful (as many would have us believe), allows us to adopt a mindset conducive to accommodating stress as a normal, healthy part of the rich tapestry of a meaningful life.

That racing heart? It's pumping blood around your body to help get you moving. Increased breathing? It oxygenates your blood to fuel your organs. And the warmth you feel is a signal that something important is happening here, that you care, and that your body and brain are getting into top gear.

Where once the myth of harmful stress would cause us to shy away from daring tasks, we can now have the audacity to take a deep breath, step in and declare: "This is my body helping me rise to the challenge of what I'm facing right now. Bring it on."

Deadlines and commitments remedy under-stress

When we don't have a deadline, we tend to be brilliant at putting things off. Under-stress lulls us into a sense of relaxed underperformance, which might feel nice for a while, but does nothing to spur us into goal-directed behaviour.

When I was completing my PhD, it felt like an endless cycle of waking, sitting at my computer keyboard, crunching numbers and writing, going to bed, then waking to repeat the process over and over *and over* again. I realised that when my deadline for a chapter or draft manuscript was two weeks or more away, my productivity was low. I could easily find distractions and would feel relief at the procrastination-avoidance behaviour, which took me away from having to focus on a big task.

It seemed that only when I was sufficiently stressed would I knuckle down, keep my bum in the seat and my fingers on the keyboard. Sometimes I would switch off my phone and close my email to help me stay focussed. I became a poster-boy for all phases of the Yerkes-Dodson Law! This boom-bust cycle of productivity became an emotional rollercoaster that would frequently see me misjudge the amount of time I needed to get everything done. I tended to underestimate how long some projects would take, and ended up feeling over-stressed with irritability and insomnia glaring at me urgently like a flashing light on an out-of-control airplane.

I needed to find a more consistent and efficient way of getting things done. So I started listing smaller goals that had to be achieved on my calendar, and my office mate Jane would do the same. If I reached my goal, I would reward myself by doing something enjoyable, like going for coffee or taking the afternoon off. By imposing artificial early deadlines for stepping stone goals and making myself accountable to someone simply by declaring this plan, I felt enough pressure to get working and stay focussed. I was able to push myself into the peak performance zone and get more done, sooner, and without later needing to feel over-stressed and overwhelmed.

When stress gets too high

Most people manage high stress poorly. Workplace and youth surveys consistently reveal that this is a major concern. Even more than wanting a "stress-free life" or seeing stress as harmful, people want help in *managing* stress. There are two key reasons why we manage high stress levels poorly:

1. we don't reliably notice when we've moved into an over-stressed state, and

2. when over-stressed, we don't do the things that mitigate stress.

In an over-stressed state, we cannot easily notice our impaired functioning and take action to resolve it. While too little stress brings with it a lack of focus, too much stress narrows our awareness to exclusively focus on the very thing causing the stress: the demanding project, the impending deadline, or the mammoth to-do list.

Before we can bring ourselves back into the optimal performance range of the Yerkes-Dodson curve we must first *recognise that we are over-stressed*. Each person has their own, unique combination of indicators that reveal when they're in the over-stressed range. I call this a stress signature.

Your Stress Signature

To recognise your stress signature, you need to first identify the unique combination of biological, psychological, and social indicators that occur when you are in the over-stressed range. Here is a list of common signs of over-stress that might be included in someone's stress signature:

- Irritability
- Sleep disturbance
- Rushing around
- Speaking faster
- Loss of pleasure / compassion / humour
- Excessive sweating
- Social withdrawal
- Fatigue
- Impaired concentration
- Muscle tension and headaches

In addition to these common indicators, you may have some idiosyncratic signs unique to your expression of being over-stressed, for example, a nervous habit such as tapping your foot a particular way. In one workshop I ran, a lady said she would clean her house as if possessed—it was her subconscious way to try to restore order and a sense of control when feeling overwhelmed by stress. When you reliably identify the signals that your stress levels are too high, you can immediately take specific actions to return to the optimal stress / peak performance range.

Life Medicines

How do we reduce stress when we're hitting the red line of the over-stressed state and our stress signature is jumping out at us? The answer lies in your life medicines. Life medicines are simple, everyday things that discharge stress: they relax and calm us, boost our mood, or help us to feel more supported. And they are the things we neglect to do when over-stressed and unaware.

Like your stress signature, these can be different for everyone. Examples of life medicines include activities like walking the dog, taking a bath, or calling an old friend. None of these seem remarkable by themselves. Doing one life medicine once might make us feel momentarily better, but is unlikely to be enough to fix our over-stressed state. Collectively, however, life medicines are a powerful individual prescription for reducing and managing stress.

When you notice your stress signature appear, pause whatever you're doing to schedule in two or three of your life medicines per week for at least two weeks. This is likely to make a major reduction to your stress levels and return you to your peak performance zone.

Of course, when the term paper deadline is looming or your boss' pet project is overdue, and you notice your stress signature so you start to schedule your life medicines… what is a common automatic thought that jumps into your mind?

I don't have enough time!

Usually we see life medicines as minor pleasures that we do when we have time, not when there are urgent, real life, important things to do. Yet they are *exactly* what's needed to return us to a state of balance. And herein lies the hidden secret of stress management: when you prioritise your life medicines, what you lose in *time* you gain back in *efficiency*. Getting back into the optimal stress range sooner means we return to being focused, clear thinking, and better able to deal with the demands of the task at hand.

My life medicines consist of several unremarkable things. Watering my garden gives me a sense of calm centeredness and gentle purpose. Oddly enough, I don't even remotely have a green-thumb. This is just one life medicine I've discovered. Others include a brisk walk at sunrise or sunset, a phone call to an old friend, cooking on my outdoor barbecue with music playing, relaxing in my spa bath. While none of these things will completely take my stress away, if done consistently, they will incrementally discharge a significant amount of stress. Like periodically releasing steam from a pressure-cooker, this gets me back to just the amount of pressure I need.

Remember, the major benefit of the optimal stress range is *efficiency*. A four-hour work day in the peak performance zone might accomplish what an eight-hour work day would when over- or under-stressed. Get stress right, and you will be working smarter, not harder.

Understanding chronic stress

One of my mentors, psychologist David Scott, loved to sketch visual representations of concepts to explain them to his clients and students. His explanation of the insidious nature of chronic stress and how it operates is one of the most useful representations I have come across.

See the graph below.

David said that when we're functioning well, and when our personal resources (energy, motivation, wellbeing) are high, we have a certain coping threshold as depicted by the horizontal line in this graph:

Through the normal course of daily life, we encounter stressors (events and problems) that we are required to cope with. When functioning well with a coping threshold that is high, we can endure the stress of the situations that life throws at us, and then return to our normal functioning.

Let's look at some examples of everyday stressors that we might encounter, represented by the four lines below: the cat gets sick and has to go to the vet, we have some short-term money problems, an argument with our spouse, and a demanding project at work.

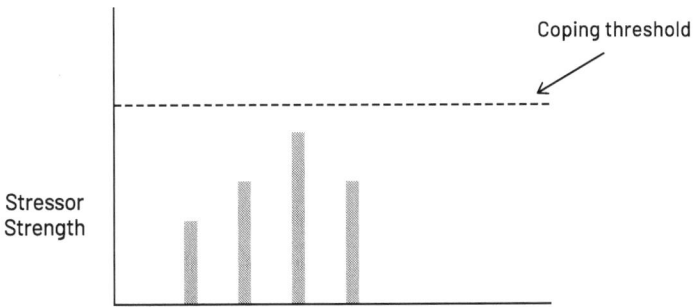

As can be seen from the above graph, each of these stress-ors falls below our coping threshold and therefore is well within our capacity to handle. That doesn't mean we won't *feel* stressed, but it will only be temporary, and it won't affect our wellbeing in any substantive way.

If, however, we encounter stressors for a long period of time without replenishing our personal energy reserves, say through taking time out or going on a holiday, doing some life medicines, or if our Wellbeing Wheel scores are low, we can end up becoming stuck in chronic stress.

What will we notice? First, we will notice that we feel over-stressed, overwhelmed, or that we cannot properly cope with the challenge (stressor) we're facing, when usually this would be something we could take in our stride. This indi-cates that our coping threshold has dropped.

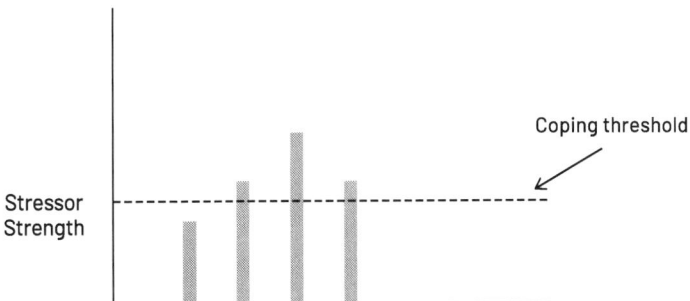

Being in the grips of chronic stress can show itself in a variety of ways. In addition to our usual stress signature, chronic stress has three general indicators that often appear in this sequence: emotional over-reactivity, loss of pleasure, and emotional numbness.

Chronic stress need not damage us or change us permanently. But it does require time, effort, and a plan to overcome. Typically, when I support clients who are recovering from chronic stress, I recommend they do the following:

- schedule in more down-time,

- reduce expectations on themselves,

- implement boundaries with others who are demanding of their time and energy,

- prioritise self-care and repairing their Wellbeing Wheel,

- identify and schedule at least 3 life medicines per week, and

- apply self-compassion (see Chapter 16).

By applying these techniques to your life during times of chronic stress, your level of emotional reactivity will return to baseline (your prior normal / healthy level) and your energy levels will be restored. You will start having the urge to do more, to start new things, and to be more socially active and engaged. It is critical to practice these techniques consistently in order to see stress levels drop and to maintain them at reasonable levels going forward. This process usually takes between 1-3 months, and sometimes longer. Ultimately, we want to find and maintain a stress range that is healthy and helps us perform well.

Harness stress and it will be your friend

Stress is an inescapable and desirable part of a meaningful, goal-directed life. Too little stress is comfortable, but could indicate that we aren't being properly challenged or living life to its full potential. Too much stress, without proper management, can overwhelm and incapacitate us.

Although formidable and sometimes intimidating, stress that is managed well will enable us to harness its power, making us bolder, braver, and able to progress further than without it.

To Do and Digest

Your Stress Signature

Take 5 minutes to reflect on those times you have been over-stressed. Think about the things you might notice about yourself, or someone else might notice about you, that would indicate you're in an over-stressed state. Ask the opinion of those closest to you in case you are unaware of some of the external signs of too much stress. Once you've compiled a list of at least 4 or 5 specific things, you will have identified your stress signature.

_____

_____

_____

_____

_____

_____

_____

_____

Your Life Medicines

Now, take a few moments to come up with at least 5 things that you enjoy, that don't take much time, effort, or planning, but help you to feel more calm, relaxed, supported, or give a boost to your mood and energy. These are your life medicines, your ready, accessible strategy for pulling back from too much stress, to just the right amount.

_____

_____

_____

_____

_____

_____

Now, when you notice your stress signature, do your life medicines.

CHAPTER 14

WHAT YOU TAKE FROM YOUR CHALLENGES WILL DEFINE YOU

Standing in front of my workshop audience, I asked the group to tell me about a challenging circumstance that had increased their capacity to face future challenges. I asked them to consider both challenges they had willingly chosen to take on as well as challenges created by circumstances beyond their control.

Importantly, I wasn't asking them if they had succeeded or not. Rather than focus on whether the outcome was "good" or "bad" or how they felt at the time, I wanted them to focus on how their *learning or development* had been positively shaped by the experience.

After some consideration, a teenage girl raised her hand.

"I was in a sailing race recently, with just me and a younger girl in the boat," she said.

"All of a sudden a storm came in, and the boat that was in charge of the safety of all the other boats ran aground on some rocks. It was really scary. I eventually managed to get us in, but it was pretty intense. I was forced to handle something I didn't think I was capable of."

She said if she'd known in advance the conditions she would have to face she definitely would have chosen to stay on the shore. But I asked if having to deal with the sailing race increased her sense of being able to handle difficult things, her self-confidence for keeping cool under pressure, and if it meant she was more willing to take on other, different challenges in the future.

"Absolutely, yes." came the reply.

My workshop participant had uncovered a vital piece of self-knowledge: that when pressed beyond her perceived limits, she could cope, resolve the difficulty at hand, and had a capability that she otherwise would not have accessed. That powerful realisation, however hard won, opened her willingness to take on challenges that required handling pressure and uncertainty (as most significant challenges do).

My point wasn't about encouraging greater risk-taking for the sake of being risky. I wanted to help my audience focus less on the outcome of their most challenging life events, to move away from the usual ledger of "good" and "bad" outcomes that tend to be the focus of many people's life narratives, and instead to see how one's psychological capacity is enhanced through the courageous facing of challenges, whether planned or not.

The key here is *willingness to face challenges*. The girl's story was instructive: her apparent misfortune from a sudden turn in the weather resulted in new levels of self-belief and courage, which in turn meant a greater scope of possibilities for her future life.

What's your willingness level?

Sitting in a meeting with a group of senior executives, I was asked to create a series of training workshops for leaders in their organisation, on a scale and size I had never tackled before. I felt I knew enough about the topic to address their needs, but what I was being asked to do was beyond anything I had previously accomplished.

I had dreamed of doing this kind of work, at this level. It would take a lot of effort to do it right, and the pressure to perform would be high. I would only get one chance to make the grade.

Natural thoughts of self-doubt crept in: *Can I really pull this off?* Although I knew I would be stepping into a world of pressure, a fair chunk of stress and some nervousness thrown in, taking this challenge on was something I *valued* more than feeling safe, calm and comfortable.

The first workshop would be the litmus test. If this went well, there would be many more. If not, my plans and reputation could come crashing down. As I addressed the large room full of expectant eyes and ears there were butterflies and sweat hidden underneath my professional exterior. At the day's end when I reviewed the anonymous feedback forms, I was relieved and excited to have delivered the most demanding and challenging workshop of my career up to that point—and it had been a hit.

The thrill and relief of success was an indication that I had achieved a new level in my professional work. But that one meeting, that one decision, opened the doorway for even greater, more exciting, and rewarding work that was to come.

When an opportunity to do something challenging arises, do you immediately imagine the exhilaration of accomplishing it, or do you list all the things that could go wrong? Do you enjoy the fine line between excitement and anxiety, the adrenaline rush of saying "yes" to something you're not 100% sure you can pull off, but would love to try? If you always find yourself coming down on the safe side of any decision, such as holding back on applying for a promotion because of the responsibility or higher stakes involved, it could be a sign that you need to expand your willingness. If you want to open up to greater possibilities in your life, next time you find your willingness to step into a challenge wavering, ask yourself these four questions:

1. Is it safe? Is it *likely* that I will be significantly damaged in some way, physically or psychologically, by taking this on?

2. If I don't think of this in all-or-nothing terms (brilliant success or abject failure), and instead imagine that I do a reasonably good job at this, will it still be a step forward?

3. Is this something I would like to do?

4. If I can accept some short-term discomfort, do I think I just might be able to handle this?

If the answer to these four questions is "yes", then take on the challenge!

No sailor controls the sea

Even the most accomplished sailor in the best boat on Earth realises that she cannot control the sea. To navigate effectively, the sailor must exert what control she has within the overall conditions, which are beyond her control. She doesn't blame the wind, the waves, or the weather; she accepts that it is part of the natural system within which she must operate. Rather than waiting for perfect conditions, she manages the tasks at hand, makes decisions, and takes reasonable action to complete her journeys in the manner that best serves her purpose and goals.

Many of the challenges that build our capability and capacity for future challenges are those we choose: starting a college degree, attempting a black belt grading in karate, pursuing a promotion. But many other challenges we face are unforeseeable, like a storm at sea. It would be easy to be intimidated by these uncertainties. If we allow the unknown to prevent us ever launching our boat, however, we will never know how it feels to truly sail. A full life, therefore, requires us to accept uncertainty and the potential for loss.

The stories we tell ourselves matter

How we view unexpected difficult times is a psychological fork in the road. One path is to draw the conclusion that life is inherently dangerous and we should seek safety. The other is to recognise that something exists within us that renders us more bold, capable, or resilient than we previously realised. As a result, our comfort zone expands, and the range of circumstances we can now take in our stride is greater than it was before. Like the young sailor's story, we can realise in ourselves a greater ability to handle challenges, to be resilient in the face of difficulty, rather than avoid challenges or seek an easier, safer path.

The tendency to label difficult times as "bad", or things not working out as "failure" is the downside of our brain's attempt at mental shortcuts. Just like the Thinking Errors discussed in Chapter 10, this kind of labelling stops us from searching out the nuanced lessons our experiences bring, the gift of a small step forward in personal development that we can find in even some of the most trying of circumstances. If we thread these labels into the narrative of our self-perception, all too often they will dampen the fire of an adventurous spirit. A person capable of so much more will succumb to the fatalistic belief: *I am what my past and my labels tell me I am.*

The degree to which we can abandon crude labels like "good" and "bad" or "success" and "failure" in the stories we tell ourselves, and instead look for the growth in each circumstance, determines the degree to which we are enriched by any experience. This way of viewing the world means all paths lead to growth. You succeed or overcome, you grow. You fail or endure difficulty, you grow.

Courage over comfort

We all have the potential to be a fearless explorer in our own life. We can reach the peak of our potential if we accept that courage is more rewarding than comfort. How many big things in the world would have been accomplished if everyone just stayed in their comfort zone? How many lucrative businesses would have been started? How many major political reforms would have been enacted? How many romances would have been embarked upon from that first nervous "hello"?

There is a false promise inherent in cautious living, because misfortune can also strike the cautious avoider. Pursuing what we value is more important than playing it safe. If we accept that some discomfort is a necessary part of that courageous path, then every obstacle is seen as an opportunity to emerge stronger and more capable than before. And a single hour of life lived in this manner can provide rewards not matched by years of timid retreat.

To Do and Digest

Have a go at finding the growth inherent in a challenge you've faced. Recall a challenging time, either from a failure, a difficulty, a misfortune, or simply from a situation that was uncomfortable.

Then, write a summary of the challenge, the growth lesson, and how you became a more capable or resilient person as a result.

The Challenge I faced was:

_____

_____

_____

_____

_____

_____

_____

_____

_____

_____

My growth lesson was:

_____

_____

_____

_____

_____

I now view future challenges as a more capable person, because:

_____

_____

_____

_____

_____

_____

The difference between being a cautious avoider or a fearless explorer comes from how we view challenges. We're about to see how the way we view something is determined by what we focus on. And this focus has consequences that go beyond just life's challenges. It permeates our view of life as a whole, with major consequences for our mood, sleep, and overall satisfaction with life.

CHAPTER 15

WHAT YOU FOCUS ON, YOU AMPLIFY IN YOUR AWARENESS

DESPITE THE EXTERNAL goings-on of the physical world around us, our mind is the filter through which all life experiences pass. Like a magnifying glass hovering over our internal states, what we focus on becomes more prominent in our attention, thoughts, emotions, and behaviours. One situation can evoke multiple different outcomes depending on the focus, because our focus directs mental, emotional, and physical energy in one direction or another.

As humans, we have a finite amount of energy. From motivation for work to personal relationships, we are using up internal reserves of personal and emotional energy as we pursue our goals. Focusing on what matters and will enhance our lives is a wiser investment than wasting time and energy ruminating over past negative events, focusing on frivolous matters in the present, or anticipating future misfortune.

Spending your energy wisely is a psychological invest-ment: it brings enhanced returns in the form of increased energy and positive emotion. If you spend it in a careless or misguided way, the return on investment is a net negative: you will be psychologically worse off. Let's take a closer look at how this works.

One of the world's leading psychologists, hypnosis and therapy expert Dr Michael Yapko, provides a powerful sum-mation of a universal truth in human psychology: "What you focus on, you amplify in your awareness". Not only does a repetitive focus on negative events, thoughts, and feelings contribute to depression, the opposite is also true. Actively cultivating a focus on what's good, our ability to solve our own problems, or the possibilities of future success, are all examples of how we can dramatically alter our experience for the better. Knowing this prompts us to be deliberate and wise in choosing what we focus on.

Consider how this principle operates in the past, the present, and the future.

Harvesting the benefits of the past: growth and gratitude

The past can provide us gifts in the present, but these gifts are not automatically provided to us. We must harvest the psychological benefits from the past. We can achieve this if we actively focus on two crucial aspects of our experience: how we've grown and what we're grateful for.

A focus on growth

In the last chapter, we learnt that challenges we face provide growth lessons. Whether categorised as a "good" or "bad" experience, there is always a lesson to be learned if we look for it. A focus on growth lessons means that regrets, disappointments, and failures can be converted into wisdom and insights that drive capability and change.

My most painful failure in early life was failing at my first chosen profession. When I was ten years old, I announced to my family that I was going to be a professional race car driver. They thought it was a childhood phase, but it wasn't. At fifteen, having saved up my pocket money from odd jobs and casual work at the local supermarket, I could finally indulge in my passion: I purchased a second-hand racing go-kart. My mother was horrified. It was old and a little rusty, but I maintained it with love and care.

I would run home from school to work on my go-kart in the shed, then simply sit in it for hours mentally rehearsing every corner and bump on the racetrack. On the weekends, I drove my heart out. I even managed to beat some of the more experienced kids who had the latest imported equipment and a family of five as their pit crew. Racing consumed my every waking moment.

Eventually, the moment of truth came. I finished high school and was ready to pursue my dream of becoming the next Ayrton Senna full time. After pleading with my parents, we brokered a deal: I could defer my acceptance to university to study psychology for a year, but if I couldn't secure racing sponsorship by the end of that year, I would have to go to university.

I couldn't find a sponsor and ran out of money. I was devastated. My dream wasn't going to come true. While it took a long time to feel at peace with this failure, I eventually realised it taught me some very important lessons:

- The value of persistence. Had I not persisted, I would never have been able to save for five years to buy my go-kart and enjoy the satisfaction and excitement of racing. This experience helped me build stamina for a long-term view of my goals at an early age.

- That I can make progress toward big goals. I learnt that even if I don't make it as far as I hope, it can be a thrill to try. I continued to dream big, because I had enough small successes to convince me I could eventually succeed at something else.

- That I can chart my own course in life. I realised I didn't necessarily need the enthusiastic endorsement of my parents (or anyone else) to try something that's important to me. Being a free thinker who doesn't need the approval of others meant being able to take action on new and different ideas.

These lessons were crucial to my later progress in other pursuits. Consciously acknowledging the benefits of my failure enabled me to make peace with the experience, and take something good from it into the future.

A focus on gratitude

Recent research has revealed substantial wellbeing benefits that come from focusing on what we're grateful for. By actively cultivating a sense of gratitude, and in particular *expressing* gratitude, there are demonstrable benefits to our mood, life satisfaction, and even sleep quality.

One powerful strategy to foster gratitude is to write and deliver a gratitude letter. It works like this:

1. Think of someone who has had a positive impact on your life, but whom you have never properly thanked.

2. Write down in detail all of the ways you benefitted from your relationship with this person, why you are thankful for them, and the impact they have had on your life.

3. Deliver the letter and read it aloud to that person.

I first learnt about this exercise at a professional development workshop with other psychologists, and the choice for me was easy: I would write a letter to my Nanna. However, we hadn't yet been told about Step 3. I believed it was simply a writing exercise to demonstrate the benefits of gratitude. It was only after writing our letters that we were told to deliver them to the subjects of our gratitude and read them aloud.

This would prove a challenge. Nanna was very old and had advanced dementia. She lived in a nursing home and seemed more frail with every visit. Nan would have good days and bad days, and I could never be sure what to expect each week when I stopped by.

It took me four or five visits to get Nan on a good day. She knew where she was, who I was, and was generally very lucid. This was my moment. I sat on the end of her bed, held her hand and read my letter aloud:

Dear Nanna,

When I was little you always made me feel safe and cared for. I perceived you to be an endless wellspring of love, affection, and food. If ever I was having a bad day, I always knew I could phone you up and you would come straight away and get me. You would whisk me off to a place where I was a prince who had anything and everything at his beck and call. You have been my constant ally and defender. You have always given me the benefit of the doubt. You have always volunteered to look after me when I have been sick, and have enthusiastically done so. I have never felt so loved without condition or restraint as when I've been in your care. Thank you so much for giving me a wonderful childhood and the most special relationship in my life.

We sat together quietly afterwards, enjoying a moment of deep connection and clarity in contrast to her usual fog and confusion. As she squeezed my hand and looked at me with her loving smile I knew how much my expression of gratitude meant to her. But the real gift was mine. Now I have a cherished memory that fills me with thanks and reminds me of the person I would like to be to others. The pain of grief has been tempered by feelings of gratitude.

Nanna passed away about a year later. I'm so glad I followed through on Step 3 of that task.

Small, regular expressions of gratitude can be powerful too, and are an excellent focus for dinner table conversations at the end of the day. In families or relationships where one person has a negative bias in their thinking and attention, this practice can be especially beneficial. It is very much possible (and important) to validate someone's bad day, to acknowledge the negative or challenging things that might be going on, but we can then ask them to identify something they are grateful for. Prompting everyone to identify something they are grateful for is a fantastic way to redress that negative bias in a way that is not invalidating or imploring them to simply think positive.

Honour the present: a focus on what's important and making the best of now

The gifts of the present moment lie in the pleasure of being absorbed in the here-and-now while enhancing what matters most. In contrast to the gifts of the past which can be "harvested" at any time you choose, your present-moment focus is a real time magnifying glass that emphasises or de-emphasises aspects of your experience. In turn this impacts the direction in which your life is going right now, as well as your immediate wellbeing.

A focus on what's important

Let's consider Jake, who focused on something that yielded no benefit to him. Jake was a pensioner who became annoyed at his new neighbour's tendency to park his car directly across the street from Jake's driveway, making it more difficult to manoeuvre his car in and out. It was a mild inconvenience, and would probably have annoyed many people, but it was not illegal.

Unfortunately, Jake became so focused on the neighbour's parking that he found himself preoccupied with it. Some days, he went to the window fifteen times to check if the neighbour's car was there. He complained to the local council and became embroiled in arguments with various council staff members who were powerless to force the neighbour to park somewhere else.

Jake attempted to rally other neighbours to support his cause until they started to avoid him, and he became openly hostile whenever he saw the offending driver. Because their previously peaceful neighbourhood had become tense and unfriendly, Jake and his wife went on fewer walks in the evening, something his wife loved to do.

Jake created unnecessary stress and anger in his life and for those around him. His focus on little annoyances meant they loomed large when they could have been forgotten. He could have accepted the annoying but minor issue of where his neighbour chose to park. Had he focused on more important and meaningful things—his relationship, a personal project, something to boost his wellbeing, or support for his local community—he would have amplified the intrinsic value they contain. He could then enjoy better mood, a healthier social life, and a sense of belonging. The outcome for Jake, his wife, and the neighbourhood, would have been much better.

You might know a Jake. You might even *be* a Jake. The lesson for the Jakes of the world is to realise that we all have a choice about what to focus on in the here-and-now. This choice magnifies our thoughts, emotions, urges, and behaviours, creating a domino effect, for better or worse.

Optimalism: A focus on making the best of now

Some people miss out on the present moment because of a persistent focus on their expectations for what's going to happen next. They focus on things needing to go perfectly (perfectionism), or expecting things to turn out well (optimism), or not well (pessimism). Instead, Harvard psychologist Dr Tal Ben-Shahar says that we should embrace the mindset of "optimalism", a focus on making the very best of whatever *does* happen.

Optimalists accept the reality that not everything is within our control, that the unexpected can and sometimes will happen, and that mistakes and failures can be of benefit to us. Because of this, they are able to enjoy the journey as well as the destination because they are not only focused on the outcome. Herein lies a willingness to be flexible. Like the Magic Question from Chapter 5, "What is the helpful thing to do now?", optimalism has no requirement for life's circumstances to turn out a particular way, but endeavours to consistently make good decisions about what to do in response to present circumstances.

The Optimalist isn't dragged down in the present by anticipating what will go wrong next, nor is he hindered by unrealistic pie-in-the-sky expectations of life and everyone around him. He is neither rigid nor obsessive because of rule-based thinking. Instead the Optimalist simply asks, "what's the best I can achieve today, with the time and resources I have available to me?".

The Optimalist is unexpectedly efficient, unflappable, and always punches above her weight. She produces delicious meals from the night-before's leftovers, and creates a captivating dress-up costume for her kids out of an old sheet, a curtain rod and painted toilet rolls. Optimalists can do the extraordinary by simply letting go. They enjoy Saturday night even when their date cancels, and realise that it's better to do what you can than lament what's out of reach.

Creating the future: A positive self-fulfilling prophecy

Our future focus influences our experience so powerfully that it can seem as if we actually create what we expect. This is demonstrated by author Pam Grout in her book *E-Squared: Nine Do-It-Yourself Energy Experiments That Prove Your*

Thoughts Create Your Reality. In the first of her experiments, Grout exhorts her readers to ask for a sign from the universe (or what she calls "FP", for the Field of Infinite Potentiality) to "prove" that it is responsive to their requests. The reader must be open-minded, and look for evidence of a sign arriving within 48 hours, but is not allowed to specify what the sign will be. She emphasises that they must look earnestly:

> "...be vigilant in receiving evidence. Look for it the same way you'd look for a set of missing car keys. On a day you're out of milk and the baby's crying. After looking everywhere you normally put them—in your purse, in the pocket of your khakis, on the counter by the door— you start lifting up couch cushions, crawling under the bed, and sifting through kitty litter. The important thing is, you don't stop looking until you're clutching them in your grubby little paws."

Grout gives examples of suitable evidence of a sign as getting a dollar-an-hour pay rise, a friend giving you a gift, or someone calling and offering to help you move house. Grout's critics have stated that her criteria for success of the thought experiment are so broad, and therefore the bar is set so low, that it is simply an example of a *self-fulfilling prophecy*: a prediction that directly or indirectly causes itself to become true.

I'm not a quantum physicist, so I won't be offering an opinion as to whether our will can alter particles of matter and manifest what we desire, except to say they we *do* create our reality in our minds. Rather than wait for others—or the universe—to respond to our wishful, focussed attention, we can instead try to notice favourable aspects of ourselves.

Creating the reality of you

What if, instead of seeking a sign that the universe is responding to our ultimatums, we looked for evidence of our own strengths and worth? These self-beliefs greatly influence our attitudes and behaviours, and therefore influence major life outcomes. I recommend that we look for evidence that proves our positive attributes.

We can observe self-fulfilling prophecies in our own behaviour: by expecting particular outcomes, we make those outcomes more likely. If my friend at work tells me he thinks my gorgeous co-worker across the hall is interested in me, I will instinctively pay her more attention, smile, and interact in a friendly, warm manner. In turn, I come across as more likeable, and she says yes when I ask her out for a coffee date. The outcome I expected happened *because* I expected it.

Self-fulfilling prophecies don't only work in our favour, however. They can work against us, too. If I'm certain I'm going to bomb out on my upcoming exam, my motivation to study is low (because what's the point anyway?), and because I don't study enough, I fail. Or I get so over-stressed at the prospect of my impending failure that I can't focus, and I bomb out. Either way, my expectation creates my reality.

So how can we apply the self-fulfilling prophecy to our advantage and create more of those good outcomes? Specifically, the most powerful application of a positive self-fulfilling prophecy is when it destroys a persistent self-defeating belief. Noticing your strengths, virtues, and effectiveness, will fortify the explicit beliefs that manifest the best version of yourself.

Belief perseverance

In the fable of the drowning man, a deeply religious man finds himself stranded on a rooftop in a flood with the waters rising around him. He is offered a rope from the higher balcony of a nearby building so he can pull himself to safety.

"No thank you, God will save me," he replies.

As the water rises further, a good Samaritan in a boat comes past and yells over the roar of the floodwaters for him to climb aboard.

"No thank you, God will save me."

The man is then forced to perch high upon the apex of the roof when a helicopter appears and lowers a ladder, ready to whisk him to safety.

"No thank you, God will save me."

Eventually, he is washed away and drowns. Arriving in heaven the man is incredulous and demands of God: "I believed in you and prayed to you. Why didn't you save me?"

God replied: "I sent you a rope, a boat, and a helicopter. What more did you want?"

This is an example of belief perseverance. Because the man held such a strong view that God would not manifest to him in any ordinary way, he could not see evidence that contradicted his expectations. Unlike Grout's "energy experiments", the man's expectation was too narrow, causing him to miss three manifestations of the help he was seeking.

Unfortunately, it is the painful beliefs we hold about ourselves that tend to persist more strongly. Like the drowning man, we often dismiss compelling evidence of the good things we would like to be true—especially about ourselves—even when they're right in front of us.

Making the future work for you

Want to create your own reality? Well, I'm sorry I can't promise you a Lamborghini just by expecting it to arrive. But what I can do is tell you how to apply a similar idea for huge advances in your self-concept and wellbeing: identify the positive opposite of the most painful and limiting belief you hold about yourself, then be unrelenting in your search for evidence that confirms the self-affirming belief. Look for any practical scenario that would provide an opportunity to gather this evidence.

Relentlessly compiling evidence that confirms your best expectations for yourself has the power to smash apart previously held beliefs that hurt and limit you. By focusing instead on self-affirming events and observations, you will create bright expectations for yourself, which in turn bring about fortuitous outcomes. Spending your energy wisely in this way is an investment which will yield better mood, overall wellbeing, and performance. Ultimately, you have the power to create a wonderful future.

To Do and Digest

Choose your focus

Amplify your awareness of gratitude for the past, optimalism in the present, and evidence for your ability to create a new, better version of yourself.

For the past: Write and deliver a gratitude letter.

Think of somebody who has had a positive impact on your life, but whom you have never properly thanked. Write a letter to them detailing what you are grateful for, and all the ways you have benefited from their influence or help. Deliver the letter in person and read it aloud or if that's not possible, call them and read it over the phone.

For the present: Practice optimalism.

At regular intervals in your day, stop and ask yourself *What can I do right now to make the best of my present circumstances?*

For the future: Create the reality of your best self by looking for evidence that confirms positive self-beliefs.

What's your most unhelpful belief about yourself? You have 48 hours to find evidence which instead supports the positive opposite.

First, identify the belief that has been limiting you the most.

Second, create a short-term, real-word scenario that reflects the positive opposite of that limiting belief. Remember: what we focus on, we amplify in our awareness. So, we need to focus instead on what we *want* to have. If we keep focusing on the limiting belief, it will loom large instead. We are looking for *any example* of the positive opposite of that limiting belief.

Then, with all the intensity of a detective in need of a promotion, look thoroughly and persistently for evidence to prove it.

For example:

Unhelpful belief	An example of a positive opposite scenario	Evidence for the positive opposite within 48 hrs
I am unlovable	Someone will pay attention to me	When I was grocery shopping a young man smiled at me as I passed him in the aisle. I received a Facebook message from an old school friend. My mother called to see how I was.
I can't do anything right	I get something done	I paid my bills on time. I cleaned out the attic. I helped my neighbour set up their new TV.
I have no control over my life	I can influence an outcome	I decided to take the bus to visit my friend rather than the train. I asked for a better price when I bought my new bed and got a discount.
I'm worthless	I am of value to someone	My workmate thanked me for my support on a project. My dog loves it when I take her for a walk & give her affection.

Repeat this process until your evidence has "proven" the positive opposite of the beliefs that have been holding you back. You might be surprised at how rapidly the new, more empowered you starts manifesting better outcomes in all areas of your life!

Thankfully, the most potent manifestation of help in your life doesn't rely on the universe, God, or a Field of Unlimited Potential. You already have it, staring you in the face every morning....

CHAPTER 16

YOUR MOST IMPORTANT RELATIONSHIP IS THE ONE YOU HAVE WITH YOURSELF

ONE AFTERNOON WHEN I was about fourteen years old, I walked home from school in a state of angst. I'd had several bad days in a row. I was on the outer with my friends, frustrated by all the challenges of being a teenager and just trying to find my place in the world.

When I got home, I threw my schoolbag down and plonked myself on the couch feeling stressed, tired, and alone. I switched on the TV, aiming to relax for a while before grudgingly starting my homework. For some reason, the TV was tuned to a local community station. When I was a kid these channels were run by volunteers and usually not many people watched them. The program looked like a very old rerun. It seemed to be just a man reading from a book.

Well, this is boring I thought, and went to change the channel. But just as I was about to switch stations, I heard the man read out loud:

"You do not need to be loved—not at the cost of yourself. The single relationship truly central and crucial in a life is the relationship to the self. It is rewarding to find someone whom you like, but it is essential to like yourself. It is quickening to recognise that someone is a good and decent human being, but it is indispensable to view yourself as acceptable. It is a delight to discover people who are worthy of respect and admiration and love, but it is vital to believe yourself deserving of these things. For you cannot live in someone else. You cannot find yourself in someone else. Of all the people you will know in a lifetime, you are the only one you will never leave nor lose. To the question of your life, you are the only answer. To the problems of your life, you are the only solution."

It turns out he was reading from one of the first ever personal development books, *Advice From a Failure*, by Jo Caudert. And as fate would have it, these were just the words my fourteen-year-old self needed to hear. I realised I had consistently been judgemental and harsh towards myself in a way that I *wasn't* to the people around me. It suddenly occurred to me:

I'm stuck with myself.

I can't run away from myself. I can't break-up with myself. Rather than be this harsh self-critic who was first to pile on judgements and derisory comments when I'd stuffed up, I actually had a choice to treat myself kindly. It was a revelation.

After years of listening attentively to my clients as they reveal their innermost thoughts, I have come to realise that many people are horrible to themselves. So often the level of criticism, hard-heartedness, and judgment that people apply to themselves in no way reflects the way they would treat others.

Jo Caudert's startling truth that we are the only ones we will never leave nor lose is a powerful reminder that we're stuck with the voice in our head. That voice belongs to us. If we are relentlessly playing the role of a critical coach, deriding our inevitable mistakes and vulnerability and never being encouraging or forgiving, the outcome is at best going to be a feeling of shameful lack. Not only does this kind of coaching lead to poor performance, it leads to low mood and a lack of confidence.

Consider instead the scenario of someone you love and care deeply about. Or even a professional colleague whom you respect. If they made a mistake, performed less than was expected, or were having a difficult emotional time for whatever reason, how would you treat them? What would you say or do to help them through it? These key questions activate one of the most important psychological concepts ever: self-compassion.

What science says about self-compassion

Professor Kristin Neff is one of the key people to bring the idea of self-compassion from the depth of Buddhist practice and into the mainstream psychology literature. Her excellent book *Self-Compassion* teaches crucial lessons about the components of self-compassion and how it works. The three main practices that cultivate self-compassion are:

1. increasing self-kindness and reducing harsh self-judgement,

2. seeing difficult or painful emotional states as part of our common humanity, rather than something that isolates us, and

3. having a mindful awareness of these emotional states, and how we respond to them, rather than being consumed by them.

In developing the *Healthy Minds* program, we conducted one of the first large-scale studies measuring self-compassion in young people. We found that self-compassion was a robust predictor of mental health: people who were higher on self-compassion, on average, tended to be lower on symptoms of depression, anxiety, body-image concerns, and unhelpful perfectionism. Self-compassion is becoming widely regarded as one of the most potent protective factors in mental health, which is why it is the subject of burgeoning research efforts around the world. Where once self-esteem (feeling good about how you evaluate yourself compared to others) was thought to be the healthiest of attitudes toward the self, self-compassion is now miles ahead. If I had to choose only one for myself—either self-compassion or self-esteem—self-compassion wins every time.

The power of self-compassion

When at work one day recently, I spilt my drink everywhere in the lunchroom. Instinctively I loudly scolded myself: "You idiot!" Then I started laughing. It occurred to me that if a colleague of mine had spilt something in the lunchroom there's no way I would have yelled at them and called them names! My self-compassion was definitely better than my fourteen-year-old self but I knew then I still had a way to go.

At other times, self-compassion has been the difference between tense frustration and calm acceptance in a busy, stressful day. At one school, I was working intensely with staff, parents, and students over three days. I had travelled a long way to be there, was jetlagged, exhausted from the long days of presenting, and to top it all I could feel a head cold coming on. One of my last presentations was in an auditorium containing more than 600 high school kids and their teachers. How was I going to muster the energy? As the auditorium manager clipped the lapel microphone to my suit, I noticed some automatic thoughts:

How am I going to get through this?
You're too fatigued, your energy level is too low.
You haven't prepared enough.
This is a big audience to go in unprepared.

Only a few moments before the doors to the auditorium swung open to swarms of students moving in, I closed my eyes to get some relief from the bright stage lights that were burning down on me and took a deep breath. A peaceful calm slowly spread through my body and mind. For a moment I felt strangely comforted and protected as if wrapped in a protective hug as another familiar voice broke into my awareness:

You're doing a great job, and on so little sleep.
This doesn't need to be perfect to get your message across.
Your message will speak for itself. Think of all the kids who will be helped by this.

This is what you do best. Go get 'em!

My self-compassionate inner voice provided a calm, steady surge of energy that arrived just in time for me to give one of the best presentations of my visit.

How do you treat yourself?

So far we have discussed the impact of our thoughts and our focus, on how we feel. It should come as no surprise, then, that saying unpleasant things to ourselves that we would never say to others can seriously impair the quality of our emotional lives.

The upside is that if we can actively cultivate the helpful alternatives: kindness, forgiveness, compassion, encouragement, and acceptance, then apply them to the way we relate to ourselves during the challenges of daily life, we will be inviting the warm presence of a dear supportive friend... ourselves.

To Do and Digest

Self-compassion in practice

Applying self-compassion requires us to train our brains. Just as using the Helpful Thinking Process helps train our brains through writing and exploring different perspectives, there are methods for training ourselves to be more self-compassionate.

One method is to keep a self-compassion journal, writing one message of self-compassion each day.

Another method, as Neff recommends, is to imagine a wise, kind, compassionate being, a being who knows everything about you and whose advice is wrapped in loving care, forgiveness, and acceptance. Hold in your mind the thing that currently makes you feel ashamed, insecure, or not good enough, take a few breaths in a quiet moment and imagine the words that flow from this compassionate mentor. It is best to write out your answer. Just like the Helpful Thinking Process, it is harder to do it in our heads than by writing it out, especially when new to this practice. Remember, writing is a great way to train our thinking.

Yet another way of enacting self-compassion is to simply apply the questions mentioned above:

> *Think about someone you care deeply about, or even a professional colleague whom your respect. If they made a mistake, performed less than was expected, or were having a difficult emotional time for whatever reason, how would you treat them? What would you say or do to help them through it?*

This immediately causes us to look outside of ourselves. Getting outside of our usual perspective will stop any autopilot self-criticisms. With the autopilot turned off, we can find a response that is kind and compassionate. Showing ourselves that same compassion we readily give to others will give us ready access to encouragement, support, and forgiveness—all things that make us lighter, brighter, more courageous, and more quickly able to bounce back.

CHAPTER UPGRADE

Get your printable copy of the inspirational
Jo Caudert self-compassion quote at:

www.tomnehmy.com/applesupgrades

CHAPTER 17

ASK FOR HELP WHEN YOU NEED IT

It seems self-evident that when you need help, you should ask for it. Yet I have seen *countless* examples over the years, literally hundreds of people, who would clearly have benefitted from asking for help but did not.

This includes the parents who waited until their child's behaviour was out of control before they sought professional input, by which point he was looking more like a jailbird-in-waiting than a kid who needed a time out. Or the stressed businesswoman who spent months procrastinating about the closing of her latest venture assuming her shareholders would be hostile to the decision. Or a husband who desperately wanted his wife's support in resolving a family conflict, but who could never quite find the right time to raise the matter, and so suffered in silence.

The end result of not asking is that the difficulty worsens, feels entrenched or helpless, and, as time passes, we become needlessly consumed with stress and fatigue when the problem could have been resolved much sooner.

Being human

There are many possible reasons for why we don't reach out and ask for help:

- Embarrassment: if we admit our struggle, we worry that we'll be seen as less than the image we portray.

- Pride: if we admit our struggle, we might need to admit a personal flaw that challenges our view of ourselves.

- Not seeing alternatives: we're on automatic pilot and have not used our thinking skills to consider a possible solution.

- Devaluing the importance of our own needs: we feel unworthy of another's time or effort, or we regard our needs as less important than others' needs.

- Emotional avoidance: it is too confronting, uncomfortable, or distressing to admit our problem.

One reason we should ask for help stands out among all others: our common humanity. Being human means being imperfect. As we discussed in Chapter 16, self-compassion is an enormously powerful wellbeing factor. Treating ourselves kindly requires us to suspend harsh self-judgement, to see the ways in which we share vulnerabilities with our fellow humans, and to not allow emotional states and problems to define who we are.

No human has ever lived without vulnerability. No human has survived without the care and assistance of another. Just because we become less vulnerable as we develop and grow doesn't mean we become free of the need to be assisted by others.

No matter how well we play the roles we are familiar with, we will still make mistakes and face circumstances outside our control. We will all require someone's input to counteract either our personal deficits or an unfortunate series of events.

Your martial arts instructor may fear little in terms of his personal safety, but may be a terrible financial manager. Your psychology professor might be a highly accomplished scientist and teacher, but put him in a desert next to a broken-down car with no GPS and he's as needy as anyone else. Wonderful, capable people frequently can and do struggle with some aspect of their lives, but this does not diminish the quality of their character.

Accepting our vulnerabilities and limitations need not degrade our strengths, and accepting this removes many of the obstacles to seeking help.

Furthermore, when you take action to help yourself, you free up mental and emotional energy that can be directed in other, more prudent ways. The energy that was consumed by the problem is then available to be invested in other aspects of life and can have positive effects that will ripple out into the future. What is good for your wellbeing is usually good for those around you, too.

Notice how rare it is to find big success in isolation from others. Peak performers rarely (if ever) reach their goals without support from coaches, mentors or assistants. If you look at the most successful business or sports people today you might notice that their ability to rally the support of others is often a key ingredient to their success, over and above their natural talents and personal goal seeking.

None of us go it alone, and the solution to what concerns *you* may be closer than you think.

To Do and Digest

Make a plan right now to tackle your most stubborn, urgent, or seemingly intractable problem. What is the first step? Who would be the most qualified or suitable person to seek assistance from? Ask yourself the Magic Question: *What is the most helpful thing to do now?*

Whether solving a problem or getting to the next level of your personal development, seeking support can save abundant time and energy. If in need, ask. The person asked is usually flattered and willing, in turn making you the grateful receiver who can stride forward to spread your unfettered energy out into the world and the future.

Finding the help you need

- What challenge are you facing in your life right now that is most causing you to feel stuck?

- What are you avoiding because of fear, worry, or anxiety?

- What is the one problem that, if solved tomorrow, would feel like a major weight has been lifted from your shoulders?

- Who do you know, or know of, who has the knowledge or expertise to help you with your most significant obstacle right now? Or who do you know or know of who could help you identify that person?

- What is the next big step forward in your personal

or professional life that can be accelerated by the involvement and input of someone else? Who would that helper or mentor be?

CHAPTER 18

YOU ARE MORE POWERFUL THAN YOU THINK

FOR ME, ADOLESCENCE was characterised by uncertainty, self-doubt, and a powerful yearning for the endless possibilities and freedom that adulthood represented. One particular day at school, I was walking along the balcony of a row of classrooms, deep in my own world (as I often was), when my English teacher, Mr Grant, hurriedly stepped out from a doorway, walking alongside me as he cradled a stack of papers and folders.

"Ah, Tom, I've just finished marking your assignment," he said breathlessly, looking at me with a gleam of expectation, searching for a reaction.

My fifteen-year-old self didn't provide one.

"Your piece was insightful, it captured my attention, and you have a real clarity of expression. Well done. But it's just what I have come to expect from a capable student like you."

With that Mr Grant smiled and darted off down a stairwell and left me, my reverie broken, pondering the possibility that I was capable and insightful. The conversation has stayed with me ever since. My fifteen seconds with Mr Grant caused me to see myself differently. My altered self-concept, in turn, would go on to shape future decisions, and therefore, experiences.

Have you ever stopped to think just how far your influence reaches? What if we could observe the journey of each decision's ripple out into the world, each piece of wisdom that lifts someone's sprit, every harsh word that leaves someone cold? The truth is, our influence goes far beyond what we ever get to see or measure. Like air and gravity, the invisibility of our interpersonal influence doesn't render it any less important or powerful.

Some people who have reported near-death experiences say that when we die we review our entire life like a movie, but we get to experience the effect of our actions from the point of view of those whose lives we touch, whether in good or not-so-good ways. Every emotion caused, every problem solved, every knotted fear we contributed to or soothed away.

Sound scary? What would your life's movie say about you? What would it feel like, from others' point of view?

In the movie *Sliding Doors,* we see two possible futures for the male and female lead characters, either together or apart, played out as alternate realities resulting from a split-second decision. Unlike watching the movie, we cannot know the differences between a multitude of possible effects cascading out from one action over another in any given moment. But knowing that our reach extends far beyond the present moment in time and space where our consciousness seems to reside, brings a sober sense of responsibility with an awareness of a power we never knew we had.

Our decisions, actions, words and emotions *will* influence others. Social psychologists have known for decades how our mere presence in a room causes others to act in ways they would not if they were alone. And not just in a "Should I scratch my bum?" way, but in a way that alters responsiveness to emergencies, likelihood of criminality, and deference to authority, to name just a few. The question then is not "Am I influencing others?", but "In which way do I influence them, and is my influence of benefit?"

Like my teacher's encouragement at a time when I was more critical of than believing in myself, interpersonal influence can echo into the future, literally multiplying its effect beyond the time and space where it began. Mr Grant's influence multiplied throughout my life.

The Multiplier Effect

In economics theory, the Multiplier Effect is a measure of consumer spending. Literally, the number of times a spent dollar is "multiplied" through the spending it generates in an economy. Let's look at how this works, because it has important implications for how we see ourselves.

Consider Judy purchasing a new tablet computer for $500.

Name	Spent	Saved
Judy	500	

She buys the tablet from Dan, and he chooses to save $100 of the $500 he's received, but goes on to spend $400 on some new speakers for his car.

Name	Spent	Saved
Judy	500	
Dan	400	100

Trudy sells the car stereo speakers to Dan and goes on to spend $350 of the cash she has received on jewellery she buys from Alison.

Name	Spent	Saved
Judy	500	
Dan	400	100
Trudy	350	50

Alison spends $300 that she received from Trudy on a new BMX bike for her son, which she buys from John.

Name	Spent	Saved
Judy	500	
Dan	400	100
Trudy	350	50
Alison	300	50

Finally, John saves $50 and then then spends the remaining $250 on some sports equipment from Roger, who happens to be a spendthrift, and saves the lot. If we follow the trail of money (and spending) from Judy all the way until the money is no longer flowing in the economy and generating short term spending (i.e., it is saved), we notice something quite compelling.

Name	Spent	Saved
Judy	500	
Dan	400	100
Trudy	350	50

Name	Spent	Saved
Alison	300	50
John	250	50
Roger	0	250
Total spending	*$1800*	

The initial act of Judy spending $500 has led to $1800 worth of spending. This is compelling because is also demonstrates the interpersonal currency of our daily lives: our *influence*. Whether consciously aware of it or not, we each weave an invisible thread of emotions, energy, decisions, beliefs, intentions, desires, inspirations, and regrets. The Multiplier Effect shows how our influence goes far beyond what we can ever see or measure.

We cannot know the future. But knowing that the currency of our influence *will* be spent or saved to the betterment of detriment of others renders each decision more valuable. Where will that dismissive sigh end? What are the consequences of the rushed goodbye, the phone message unreturned? Or alternatively, the attentive pause in a breath when you ask someone "how are you?" and you really care about the answer? In such a complex array of possibilities, how are we able to understand what the consequences might be?

Near death survivors who describe the life review point not only to the practical implications of what we say and do, but the prominence of the emotions associated with our words and actions. In the life review, the emotional undertone and intent of any given action resonates as strongly as the action itself.

Emotional labour

Emotions are contagious. Consider the person you meet whose enthusiasm and excitement makes you feel excited too. Or the complaining friend who always has a tale of woe that leaves you feeling drained and flat. Emotional contagion occurs all the time in our interpersonal interactions.

Emotional contagion is not only apparent in our close interpersonal relationships, but also in superficial interactions. Have you ever had the experience of going into a store and the shop assistant asks you how you are, but with a tone and body language that tells you he *doesn't give a shit?* Another shop assistant on another day might address you with the same question, but with a warmth and demeanour that leaves you feeling there is a genuine interest in your experience of being there. Same words, different emotion conveyed. This is known as *emotional labour*. Emotional labour refers to the work we put in to our emotional displays, but remember our emotions also work on our behalf: they affect others after they receive the feeling we project, whether effortful or unconscious.

People who work in service industries know that emotional labour is part of doing the job well. Sociologists have studied this phenomenon closely in the cabin crew of airlines. A big part of their professional role is to make sure their customers feel comfortable and relaxed in a situation that is not comfortable and relaxing (in economy class at least). If they've had a fight with their partner, have money worries, or didn't get much sleep, they still need to have a winning smile and warmth that puts the passengers at ease. In this sense, emotional labour can be costly: it takes effort and energy. But it pays off in the enhanced emotional state of others.

How does your influence make others feel?

Any good child psychologist will tell you that the adults in a home set the emotional tone of the house. If they are well, balanced, and calm, the children will tend to be too. If the parents are frequently over-stressed, this will typically manifest in ratty, challenging behaviour in the kids, because kids pick up on their parents' emotions. Likewise, we send out an emotional wavelength in any environment in which we interact with others. You are the radio transmitter at the centre of your universe, what frequency do *you* want to transmit?

If underlying emotions and intentions matter as much as external words and actions, and knowing our influence is multiplied out into the world around us and into the future, then don't we have a responsibility to project a benevolent emotional influence to those souls caught within the net of our influence, and beyond?

How to be a curious listener

A study examining predictors of successful outcomes in therapy for depression compared ratings of the strength of rapport between therapists and their clients (known as the *therapeutic alliance*) and how well the therapists adhered to the treatment protocol (in other words, if they did the therapy correctly). Stunningly, researchers found that the strength of the therapeutic alliance was a better predictor of client recovery than the therapist doing the treatment correctly! Psychologists then knew that while interpersonal skills are not psychological skills *per se*, they absolutely have a psychological impact on client success.

And your interpersonal skills will have an impact on your relationship success, whether the relationship is lifelong or fleeting. Strengthening your rapport—your connectedness—with the people you love, work with and interact with day to day, will enhance the influence you have and therefore your potential positive impact on the world around you. Developing rapport with people facilitates influence, understanding, openness to suggestion, familiarity, and acceptance.

The strength of the invisible thread of rapport is based on understanding and empathy. Building understanding and empathy usually does not occur automatically but emerges from specific building blocks of communication. I refer to using these building blocks as being a *curious listener*. A curious listener does not interact with others on automatic pilot, in which asking "how are you?" is a social norm rather than a genuine question. A curious listener will:

- ask open questions,

- be present, and

- use reflections to validate and check for understanding.

Open questions are questions that do not simply require a one-word answer. Rather than saying "Did you have a good weekend?", a curious listener will ask "How was your weekend?" or "What did you do over the weekend?" Open questions invite an elaborate, rather than superficial, answer, and provide rich information upon which we can express empathy and build understanding.

Being present means not anticipating the answer, or planning what we are going to say or do next, but waiting to see, feel, and hear what the other person's experience is. Being present offers respect to the subject of our attention and creates the space for us to connect, for the invisible thread to grow. True empathy and understanding cannot occur if our attention is not on the present moment.

Reflections are about validating and checking that we have correctly understood the other person's point-of-view. A curious listener is never content to assume they understand the other person. They will always check for understanding.

Being a curious listener is powerful

One of the first clients I saw as a young, newly registered psychologist was an older gentleman who had arrived in Australia from a war-torn country. He had some symptoms of posttraumatic stress and depression. Now, at this stage of my career, I was not doing particularly sophisticated therapy. And this man could have been forgiven for questioning how a young, unworldly person such as I could be able to help or advise him. So I told the man, "I will not presume to know anything about you or your experience, but I will promise to give you all my attention to learn as much as I can from what you have been through to see if I can help."

Throughout our sessions, I used reflections like, "I imagine that this affected you by...." or "It sounds like that was...." The man would either nod and elaborate, at which point our rapport deepened, because he could see I was listening and understood, or he would clarify and correct me, and our rapport would deepen because now he *knew* I understood.

By checking for understanding, all roads led to greater rapport, deeper connectedness, and a more powerful therapeutic alliance. I didn't just understand my client, I *showed* him that I understood—a subtle but very powerful difference.

When our final session came I was feeling rather pleased with myself. My client's symptoms had subsided. I made some final notes as the appointment came to a close and was silently congratulating myself on having done such a good job, when I looked up from my notepad to see him quietly crying.

Momentarily stunned by his tears, I asked him what he was thinking and feeling, to which he replied, "This is our last time together, and I am crying because this is the first time in my life that anybody truly understood me."

My ability to diligently use the simple skills of being a curious listener fostered a powerful strength of rapport, forming an unlikely connection between two people of wildly different backgrounds, circumstances, and outlooks. In just a few short hours of conversation, my client was mourning its loss.

The Wellbeing Wheel tells us that strong, healthy relationships with others are crucial to our overall wellbeing. And our wellbeing is the engine that drives our functioning and performance. When you master the skills of being a curious listener who is truly prepared to swim around in another person's worldview, you'll find you have a greater impact on those around you. The strength of your multiplier—the power operating through the Multiplier Effect of your influence—will increase. When you interact with others:

- You can put them at ease.
- They will be drawn to you.
- You will be better liked.
- You will have more credibility.
- They will be more responsive to you.
- You can challenge them.

- You can powerfully disagree.
- You can guide their thinking.

We do not need to like someone or share their values in order to be a curious listener and build rapport. In fact, anybody in a position of management, leadership or counselling and advising, will know that professional ethics dictates we cannot only work with those whom we like. We cannot only support (professionally at least) those with whom we share the same interests and values. In personal relationships, being a curious listener means we can enhance the existing positive foundation of care and goodwill. Your partner will feel heard, appreciated, and valued.

In the absence of genuine rapport, empathy, and understanding, we cannot hope to effectively manage, assist, or deeply connect with others. One of the benevolent by-products of increased interpersonal effectiveness is that when you build rapport with someone, whether a workmate, client, spouse, or child, you will be better able to help them shape positive self-beliefs.

The Architecture of Belief

One of the strategies I often teach parents of kids in therapy is to engineer a situation in which the child overhears them talking to someone else, perhaps on the phone, in which they remark at how impressed / excited / pleased they are that a change in their child's behaviour has taken place. Even if that change in behaviour has only *started* to take place, the third-person feedback will powerfully influence the child's self-concept. Hence, the child who believed he was a naughty child would start to see himself as a "sometimes well behaved" child, or a child who "used to find it hard to behave well but now is more mature and sensible."

Children have a highly fluid, under-developed sense of self and identity and are therefore very responsive to suggestions about themselves. Adults tend to have a better formed sense of personal identity, but are nevertheless susceptible to changes in their self-beliefs through feedback. Feedback informs beliefs in powerful ways.

If I am unsure about beliefs such as: "I am capable", or "I am likable", my beliefs about myself will strengthen one way or the other based on the feedback I receive. If Mr Grant had told me I had received an average mark and he had expected this of me, I would have slumped away in disappointment and established low expectations for my future grades. But fortunately, my ambivalence was met with praise, and Mr Grant's enthusiasm for my expected good work bolstered my expectations of myself.

You can be the Mr Grant to others. You have opportunities every day to send out the gift of your underlying emotion and intent (warmth, a smile, a handshake) while engaging your curious listening skills. By deliberately noticing, reflecting, and emphasising strengths and positive attributes in others, you can shape their beliefs about themselves, which can in turn influence their behaviour.

The invisible thread you weave between yourself and those around you will greatly increase your interpersonal influence: opportunities to sow seeds of positive self-beliefs that multiply and grow into better futures. Then, what you notice, suggest, and share with others will ripple and flow outward in your quiet, persistent, benevolent wake.

To Do and Digest

Emotional balance and wellbeing are fostered through strong, healthy relationships with others. Peak performance in any domain of life requires us to fulfil our interpersonal potential, influencing others in helpful, impactful, and memorable ways. Use the checklist below as a guide for strengthening the invisible thread of your rapport in your daily interactions. A good plan for implementation is to do one strategy, once, every day. Move through the list of building blocks one at a time and soon you will find you are naturally building powerful connections with everyone around you.

The building blocks of rapport:

☑ Use emotional labour	Be conscious and effortful in the emotions you display to others. How you say something matters as much as the words you use.
☑ Ask open questions	Questions starting with "how", "why", or "what" lead to more elaborate answers than when we presume the response will be simply yes, no, or a single word answer.
☑ Be present	Rather than anticipating the answer or preparing the next thing you're going to say, really *listen*.
☑ Use reflections to check for understanding	It's not enough to understand. True rapport comes from communicating understanding. Reflect back what you heard, in your own words. The storyteller will either confirm that you understand them, or they will clarify and then know that you understand.

CHAPTER 19

DO WHAT MATTERS (TO YOU)

After working for years as a palliative care nurse, Bronnie Ware had spent a lot of time listening to people's life stories. At the end of their lives, Bronnie's patients were often immobile, contemplative, and grateful for her presence. Often the only thing they were able to do was reminisce on their life's journey, including all the moments they savoured, and their occasional regrets.

When facing death, Bronnie's patients had done away with all pretence and impression-management, something that preoccupies so much time and energy of younger, healthier people. In these moments, she would listen to the brutally honest, often peaceful reflections on what had mattered most to them. Over the years, Bronnie observed a pattern, a common theme, amongst the regrets that people expressed in their dying days. Her excellent book *The Top Five Regrets of the Dying: A life transformed by the dearly departing* details these themes.

The number one regret?

I wish I'd lived a life true to myself, not the life others expected of me.

All of a sudden, when there was no time left, no approval to be gained, no desire to impress or placate, many people said they regretted not having made their life their own.

A life true to yourself

Living a life that others expect of us is rarely an intentional decision. Instead, we are drawn in different directions by the pressure to conform. The heavy pull of conformity pressure usually emanates from one of three prime suspects: family, peers, and our internalised ideals of what a good / happy / successful life should look like.

The first obstacle to living a life true to ourselves is our families, who are usually well intentioned. Loving families want us to be safe, secure, and happy. They want what is best for us, but it is *their view* of what's best for us. Often, the natural instinct of a parent to protect their child will remain the driving influence behind their advice and approval. It comes from a benevolent place that allays parental fears. Unlike the more temporary influence of peers, families can exert their influence throughout entire lifetimes.

Peers are the second obstacle to living a life true to ourselves; they loom large in our formative years as agents of social inclusion and acceptance. At just the time we are figuring out who we are and who we want to be, our social survival and self-worth is largely determined by others who are equally consumed by insecurity, confusion, and a desperate desire to fit in. Peer pressure can cause us to think and act in ways that do not reflect our true nature, and can therefore lead to experiences, habits, and life choices that are not our own.

It was in this melting pot of hormonal development that I learnt one of the most painful but beneficial lessons of my young life. There were times in my teen years that I felt rejected and humiliated by some of my peers. The pain of rejection brought loneliness, but it also brought a gift. I learned the hard lesson of self-reliance: I am the one person with whom I will always be present, in the pains and the joys, throughout my entire life. (And, as we've covered, it also helped me understand the necessity of self-compassion).

The lonely times also taught me the power of hopes and dreams. I focused on what I wanted to change and create for my future life. Feeling rejected because I didn't fit in taught me that nobody else's opinion is worth more than my integrity. I became more determined, more resilient, and more free. For I was no longer shackled to the cold chains of conformity. And not being constrained by the approval of others meant the ability to think, act, and feel without restraint. I had the power to disagree, to be original, to challenge the accepted norm.

Years later, I would revisit this theme while giving a parent presentation to one of our accredited *Healthy Minds* schools. A concerned parent raised her hand in the Q&A session, asking for advice on how to help her daughter who struggled with academics and sports, felt outshone by a talented older sibling, and was having a difficult time being accepted by her friends. We discussed some ideas, but then I came back to what was perhaps the most important point of all to allay the mother's concerns:

"As painful and challenging as this time is for your daughter, it could be the making of her. Many kids who are forced to do away with the social approval of others become free thinking non-conformists who learn to rely on themselves. It doesn't necessarily make the difficulties of now any easier, but this is something that could pay off later in ways she doesn't realise or expect."

The third obstacle to living a life true to ourselves is the hidden spectre of our *internalised ideals*. These are the concepts we develop throughout life of what success and happiness are all about. If we treat these concepts as important markers by which to judge ourselves, they become compelling drivers of our behaviour and life choices.

Some people judge themselves by how much money they make or if they own a big house or fancy car. In this case, the internalised representation of success is material wealth, which manifests as pursuing and prioritising the accumulation of high-status assets.

For others, personal success is about being liked by as many people as possible, which results in a striving for high-profile professional roles or social visibility.

Many people judge themselves by appearance-based goals such as body shape or weight. The ideal of attractiveness and beauty is so often represented in the media as thinness, hence the current epidemic of body dissatisfaction and unhealthy weight control behaviours in young people.

On reflection, it is easy to forgive ourselves for living the life others expect of us, because it evolves out of duty to our family, social survival at crucial junctures in our development, or diligence in pursuing goals we perceive to be important. But whether driven by family, peers, internalised ideals, or a combination of all three, if the goals we strive for are inconsistent with our most important personally held values, we experience a deep-seated psychological discomfort, sometimes referred to as "cognitive dissonance".

Cognitive dissonance is the discomfort we feel when there is inconsistency in our thoughts, beliefs, and behaviours. For Bronnie Ware's patients, this discomfort was relieved when they acknowledged their regrets with all the unfettered honesty of a deathbed confession. But you don't have to wait until the end of your life to try to resolve this inner conflict, often buried deep beneath the mundane pressures and routines of modern life. Evaluating and realigning your values and behaviour will result in an amazing harmony: the resonance of thoughts, actions, and purpose.

Values drive purpose

Being clear on our personal values and ensuring that our actions and goals hold true to these values creates a powerful fusion of purpose. Then when someone asks "What gets you out of bed in the morning? What drives you?", we'll have an answer that goes beyond the superficial comfort of conformity. We'll speak with a clarity and conviction that we wouldn't have if we were motivated by our parents, peers, or internalised ideals.

If you've never stopped to think about how much of your decision-making comes from the values or beliefs you've assumed from your parents, peers, or internalised ideals, now is the time. When our actions are driven by *our* values, we find a deep and abiding sense of personal, philosophical, and spiritual purpose that propels us forward even in the face of great challenges. It provides a sense of warm contentment even when life feels as if we're trudging against the driving snow. It allows us to live a life true to ourselves.

Do and Digest

Clarify Your Values – the Dinner Party Exercise

Living according to our values is different from being goal-driven. Goals have a specific end point, and we either achieve them or we don't. While a goal is something we want to do or achieve, a value relates to who we want to be and how we want to behave on an ongoing basis.

Here's a great exercise to help you clarify your values.

Consider the following scenario: You can invite any 5 people you like to a dinner party. It doesn't matter if it is unlikely you will ever actually get to meet or invite that person to dinner, just let your imagination run free.

On a piece of paper, or in a document, create 3 columns. Then:

1. In the left column, write down the names of those 5 people (there's no rules here, invite whomever you want).

2. Next to each name, in the centre column, write down the reasons you are inviting that person.

3. Review the reasons you are inviting that person, and then in the right column, write down that person's values (from your perspective, don't over-analyse).

4. Review the list of values and circle the values that most resonate with you.

This exercise is both simple and profound. It is truly a powerful insight that reveals your own values. Once you have your values circled, consider each one and think about the degree to which you are living in accordance with those values today. Then write down your answers to the following questions:

1. *Do you feel your work, relationships, or life in general reflect those values?*

2. *If you were living those values on an ongoing basis, would anything about your life right now need to change?*

3. *Which of your identified values do you feel you are most consistently "living" in your day-to-day actions, and which value is being expressed the least in your day-to-day actions?*

4. *Are there any circumstances, roles, or habits in your life that directly contradict your identified values?*

This exercise might confirm the harmony of values, actions, and purpose you already feel. Or, it's possible you feel a little overwhelmed by how out of whack your life and values are. If that's the case, rather than focus on the uncomfortable feelings arising from this dissonance, pick one thing you can start doing now to bring you more in alignment with your values. You may not be able to quit your job and run off to join an artist's colony like you dreamt of doing when you were twenty, but you could sign up for a pottery class to bring creative expression back into your life. Or you may be over 30 and your dreams of being a professional baseball player have passed you by, but you could join an amateur league to start enjoying sports with like-minded people.

Values like integrity, justice, and honesty seem intangible. So how can we align with these? It helps to think specifically about where in your life the dissonance arises. Are you stuck in a sales job pushing a product you don't believe in? The most helpful thing to do now might not be to walk into your boss' office and quit, but you could explore other roles within your workplace, or start some training on the side with a view to finding a job at some point that better fits with your values. The thing about values is that they are enduring, without an end point—so play the long game. Values like assertiveness, health, and kindness are more amendable to immediate change, because they are reflected in behaviours that we could engage in straight away.

If it feels like you have a way to go in order to truly live your values, remember, like all aspects of the Wellbeing Wheel, we can treat it like a project. We wouldn't expect to go from a 5 to a 9 on any of the Wellbeing Wheel segments overnight. We would need to tackle it with consistent, small, daily behaviours. This moderate consistency is the golden key to sustainable major long-term change, no matter which aspect of life we want to target. Big things always feel far away at the beginning, but with each successive step, it becomes closer and more achievable.

Living your values is an extremely powerful driving force that contributes to both your wellbeing and performance. Be clear on the most important changes you need to make to ensure your values and actions resonate. Once they do, it will feel as if your general drive for life is turbocharged, and you will naturally seek opportunities to expand your personal growth and capabilities.

CHAPTER 20

EXPAND YOUR CAPABILITIES

WELLBEING AND ACHIEVEMENT go hand-in-hand. Expanding your wellbeing, including your psychological functioning, is the *single most important factor* in expanding your capabilities, achieving your dreams, and having the life you want. The preceding chapters have established some principles that will give you a psychological edge in the everyday challenges you encounter. But now it's time to take things next level.

Once you've established a strong baseline of wellbeing and clarified your most important values, what are some strategies to reach new heights in your personal development? How do we take our *good* progress and make it *exceptional* progress?

Making a conscious decision to expand our capabilities means deliberately taking on challenges and change. Many people's personal growth happens incidentally as a result of coping with and managing life experiences that have been thrust upon them. But deliberate personal growth comes from finding a way to thrive while willingly stepping into difficult (but valuable) challenges of our choosing. Expanding our capabilities is the personal development equivalent of going to the gym. You become fitter, stronger, and able to perform at a higher level than before. Maintaining our peak performance and high functioning means we will more consistently rise to the top in whichever domain we choose.

Thriving with challenges and change

One of the great privileges of working with people at both ends of the wellbeing-performance continuum, and helping them as they move from one end to another, has been gaining insights into what drives and sustains this change. Among many contributing factors, five themes consistently appear. The five crucial lessons to reaching and sustaining exceptional performance are:

1. Focus on your **long-term development** rather than short-term emotional states.

2. Be **willing to accept** some discomfort.

3. Keep a focus on your **values and strengths.**

4. Be **systematic** in building your capabilities.

5. **Maintain your wellbeing** across all areas of the Wellbeing Wheel, but especially your psychological skills.

Let's look at each of these in turn.

Focus on your longer-term development

The obstacle I see time and time again that gets in the way of personal growth and development is what I call the *Great Mistake*. The Great Mistake is when we prioritise short-term emotional states (comfort, relaxation, boredom, relief) over what would benefit our longer-term learning and development.

It seems to me that there are two unseen forces that govern most of our decisions in life—passive and active forces—and we oscillate between the benefits and costs of each. If you look carefully at the two lists below you will get a sense for what I mean.

The Twin Forces that Govern Us

Passive Forces	*Active Forces*
Comfort	Excitement
Safety	Challenge
Calm	Stress
Respite	Discomfort
Rest	Goals
Relaxation	Risk
Ease	Effort
Boredom	Accomplishment
Letting go	Reward

The benefits of one force are at the opportunity cost of the other. We routinely move between the two in cycles that may last a day (effort and rest), months (avoiding something we would like to be able to do, but that makes us nervous), or an entire lifetime (habitual avoidance of discomfort).

When we are driven by avoidance of discomfort (short-term relief over our long-term development) we deny ourselves the chance to learn two important things:

1. That we can exceed our own expectations when we face uncomfortable situations.

2. That we will adjust when we step outside of our comfort zone.

If you turn down a promotion at work because you feel uncertain and anxious about being able to fulfil the role, you are making the Great Mistake. When you decline to go to a party because you realise nobody you know well is going to be there, you are making the Great Mistake. When you have a dream that aligns with your values and strengths, but you don't pursue it because the goal seems too big and feels like it will take forever, you are making the Great Mistake. The Great Mistake is a major barrier to making our dreams come true.

Be willing to accept some discomfort

One of the most reliable psychological processes on Earth is that of *habituation*. As we learnt in Chapter 7, if we are willing to face our fears repeatedly, in a graded way, we *will* adjust, we *will* get used to it, and eventually what made us anxious *will* become comfortable. The same process applies to building confidence and expanding your comfort zone. Doing difficult, big, and exciting things will naturally and predictably feel out of our depth when they are new, different, or at a higher level than before. This discomfort is a natural, normal sign that we are being challenged, and should not be confused with danger. Just as the physiology of fear and excitement are much the same (both involve activation of the adrenal system), it is the context that determines which is the more appropriate label and the appropriate response. If you are in danger, run. If you are nervous but safe, *step into the challenge.* The only way to avoid the Great Mistake is by accepting some discomfort in favour of personal growth.

Just telling someone to step into discomfort because they will adjust to it is not a sufficient rationale to take on a challenge. It has to fit with what they *value.* That is why experiencing discomfort to remove a problem is more common than experiencing discomfort to expand personal capabilities. Removing a significant problem has a clear, ready rationale: making life better by removing an aversive state that already exists. The comfort and safety of the passive force beckons, promising relief from the stress of the problem.

Lifelong dreams are not often prioritised in the same way as urgent problems. Expanding your capabilities requires a movement *away* from a state of relative comfort and into the wilful zone of the active force, with all the accompanying effort, risk, and stress. Someone might be happy with their middle-management job, but deep down they also want to be, do and have *more.* If they see the possibilities that would come from directing the operations of the company, and they truly believe in their work, they will actively seek out challenges that enable them to be promoted, taking on greater responsibility and influence than before.

This is why deliberate personal growth sets us apart from the many people who fatalistically resign themselves to the outcomes of the passive force. Expanding our capabilities requires experiencing discomfort to achieve a higher level of ability and success. The sustainable pursuit of difficult but important things is driven by our deep sense of purpose. It requires the courage to face the uncertain and unfamiliar, and to give up an easier and less responsible life in exchange for a more powerful, conscientious life.

Keep a focus on your values and strengths

Given what you now know about your own values, what would be a step out of your comfort zone, but that you would be willing to try? What new goal would utilise your strengths to enable you to reach a new level in your work, relationships, or other important pursuits? What challenge in your life right now, if you conquered it, would make a world of difference?

The night before one of my first major workshops, I barely slept. I felt nervous and unsure how it was going to turn out, but I really wanted to make a career out of presenting personal development and psychological skills workshops. I knew that one of my strengths was public speaking, but I had never done it on this scale before. I would be over the moon with excitement if I could pull it off and do a good job.

I went off the next morning to present the workshop on only a couple of hours' sleep, already sweating in my business suit from the pressure of the task ahead. As it turned out, the day was a success, the client ended up booking many more workshops, and soon I was looking to expand my capabilities with bigger audiences and more challenging topics.

Expanding my professional capabilities this way wasn't about feeling supremely confident or completely in control, but being willing to face the challenge because it mattered to me.

Be systematic

Tackling a fear or phobia with graded, repeated exposure involves mapping out the steps to the goal behaviour and doing each initial step enough times that it becomes easy. Building confidence and competence works in much the same way. Each involves a process of habituation, in which something that felt out of our comfort zone or prompted us to avoid it gradually becomes comfortable. Situations that once felt extraordinary and difficult become normal.

Big goals that seem out of reach become achievable when we take a systematic approach. Just looking at the top of a mountain we want to climb is intimidating and scary. But the walk to the base of the mountain, not so much. When we're at the base, the first rest stop doesn't seem so far. Eventually, by just focusing on the near goal and shifting our focus in a gradual way, the ultimate achievement naturally comes in to focus at the right time: when we have completed most of the journey and the preparations bring us within reach.

Achieving big goals isn't something only top performers do. It can be any significant thing we want to achieve, and it is normal to not feel ready, worthy, or prepared for that goal when we start. My ladder had a big goal at the top: to present to audiences in the hundreds, to be the keynote speaker at major conferences, and to reach thousands of people with my message. For me, this would represent peak performance in a field of work that was very important to me. When I was just starting out, if I shared this goal with others I might have been accused of hubris. But once I was clear about where I wanted to get to, I refocused on the first step: my first presentations to small audiences. It wasn't unexpected to me when I felt nervous; that was simply a clear sign that I was expanding my capabilities by taking a step outside my comfort zone. If that first presentation felt easy, it wasn't a challenge that would help me get to the next rung on the ladder.

When activities at the first rung of my ladder started to feel easy, it was time to take on something bigger. By following this stepwise approach, in a few short years I had reached my goal. It didn't feel extraordinary when I made that final step, it was only when I thought back to the beginning that I realised something remarkable had taken place in my personal growth. That's the beauty of this systematic approach: when achieving a momentous goal feels like just one regular step in a series of small, progressive successes, then the system has worked exactly as intended.

Maintain your wellbeing

Wellbeing is something you *do.* Wellbeing, and therefore performance, comes not from knowing what makes you well. It comes from *doing* the things that create and maintain a state of wellbeing.

No matter how much I talk about wellbeing in presentations and workshops, if I don't have a routine for checking that I am proactively applying what I know, I'm unlikely to be consistently engaging in wellbeing behaviours. We *all* tend to regress toward the average if we are on autopilot, me included.

To check if you are engaging in the wellbeing behaviours that will provide the energy and foundation for your progression up the ladder to a broader, bigger, comfort and capability zone, use the following self-reflection checklist (I recommend you download and print a copy to put on your fridge).

- *Do you regularly audit your wellbeing on the Wellbeing Wheel?*

  I make a formal practice of doing this with my business partner Nick at each of our quarterly business meetings, if not sooner.

- *Do you take small daily actions to enhance and maintain your wellbeing?*

  Small, daily actions in aid of your wellbeing are sustainable, with lasting effects over time, in contrast to large, wholesale, overnight changes.

- *Are your emotions like the weather?*

  If your self-ratings on the Wellbeing Wheel are consistently high, and your emotions are like the weather (regular experience of good mood but also experiencing negative emotions without getting stuck in a state of negative emotion), then it's very likely you're in a state of good mental health.

- *Do you maintain an awareness of your personal stress signature and where you are on the stress-performance curve?*

  Stress is neither good nor bad, it is about the right amount at the right time. Recognising when you are over-stressed is important because during these times we have lower levels of self-awareness. Be aware of your stress signature so when you notice it, you can take helpful action.

- *Do you regularly schedule in your life medicines?*

  Life medicines can be therapeutic when you're over-stressed, and they can also be a preventive strategy to keep us in the optimal stress zone. Remember, life medicines seem unimportant compared to stressful and urgent tasks, but they are necessary to bring us back into the peak performance zone. And implementing life medicines as a matter of course, an ongoing priority, can prevent the onset of your stress signature when you reach an over-stressed state.

- *Are you making good decisions, even in the face of strong emotions? Do you use the Magic Question?*

  When emotions rise up, or when you are feeling stuck, always ask: *"What is the helpful thing to do now?"*

- *Do you notice healthy vs. unhealthy thinking in yourself and others?*

  See if you can notice when someone is over-generalising, catastrophising, mind-reading, or fortune telling. Look out for anxious thinking (over-estimating risk), depressive thinking (being overly negative about the self, world, or future), or angry thinking (attributing hostile intent to others when none exists).

- *Do you use the Helpful Thinking Process whenever you feel stuck in a state of negative emotion?*

  Healthy thinking is thinking that is balanced, realistic, and helpful. By following a series of prompts to challenge and revise your automatic thoughts, you can moderate emotional reaction urges and make good decisions. Don't forget to download the Helpful Thinking Process PDF from the Chapter Upgrade at the end of Chapter 11 and save it to your computer. It is an invaluable tool whenever you feel stuck in a state of negative emotion or if you need to check your thinking.

- *Do you treat yourself kindly?*

  If you make a mistake, have a bad day, or are experiencing a difficult time, think about what you would say to or do for someone you really care about if they were in this situation. That's what you need to apply to yourself. Remember, self-compassion is a major predictor of good mental health.

- *Do you regularly practice gratitude?*

  If "what you focus on, you amplify in your awareness," why not focus on the good stuff? And remember, expressing gratitude is even more powerful than just thinking it.

To Do and Digest

To reach the next level of your personal capabilities, do the following:

Identify an area of life in which you strive for greater long-term development, but in which you are making the Great Mistake. Make sure it fits with one of your identified values from the previous chapter.

Create a drawing of a ladder, with your biggest, most meaningful goal at the top. It is totally fine if it feels strange writing out something that seems almost unattainable or unbelievable. The exciting and satisfying thing about all big achievements is that they once seemed impossible and out of reach.

Then create some steps on the ladder, say five or six, or however many seem appropriate to you, and fill them in, starting with the first rung. The first rung on the ladder is one concrete step toward that ultimate goal, and is something that would be achievable with some effort in the short-term. This rung should be one step outside your comfort zone, or your current level of achievement and capability, but something you could do if properly prepared, coached, or practised.

Then complete the remaining rungs or steps, each increasing in difficulty and expectations of yourself, until the entire ladder is complete. The second-to-top rung should be a logical step directly below the goal at the top. Now look back down to the bottom rung and make that your focus until it has become as familiar and comfortable as where you currently are now. You know what to do next: step up!

Finally, complete the wellbeing self-reflection checklist to ensure you are maintaining an optimal state of wellbeing.

CHAPTER UPGRADE

Get your free copy of the 'Are you maintaining a healthy mind?' checklist and put it on your fridge!

www.tomnehmy.com/applesupgrades

WHAT'S POSSIBLE?

IF YOU CAME across Bill Mason in the street, you would probably think him an unremarkable older man. Bill Mason, however, is anything but unremarkable. From the late 1960s to the late 1980s, Bill was North America's most notorious jewel thief. He stole millions of dollars' worth of jewels over his career. He would scan the society pages of his local newspaper to see who was being particularly ostentatious in their displays of wealth. No heist was too big or small for Bill, but it really wasn't about the money—it was about the challenge.

One particular challenge arose when Bill noticed a new apartment building complex. "Best Security in the World" it boasted, luring well-to-do retirees to the Florida coastline for a safe and secure retirement. Ironically, this also lured Bill, which meant the residents' baubles were anything but safe.

One morning, the residents awoke to find their biggest and most expensive pieces of jewellery gone. The shock reso-nated throughout the Florida community, and particularly the police who were confounded. The media headlines screamed about the "gang" of thieves or the "phantom" of whom no trace could be found.

Eventually, when Bill was arrested on an unrelated theft, unsuspecting investigators foolishly granted him immunity from prosecution if he would confess to his other crimes. The police were shell-shocked when he admitted to the Florida apartment complex heist. Eager to know how such a caper was executed, they listened intently when he walked them through it.

Having done his homework meticulously, Bill executed his plan with all the skill of a master of his craft. His strategy? Late one Saturday night, staying clear of the security cameras outside the complex, he waited for a small group of friendly-looking tipsy revellers making their way home after a night out. He said hello, greeted them with a warm smile and tucked his baseball cap low over his face, walking with the group all the way through the reception foyer, into the elevators, and up to higher floors where he alighted and went about his spree.

Bill's revelation was extraordinary. He simply walked right in. He was right there on the CCTV footage that had been pored over countless times by trained detectives.

When asked how he was able to get away with such a brazen and simple strategy, Bill's answer was profound:

"It was a failure of imagination," he said.

Nobody, not the police, the residents, or the security, could conceive of the thief simply walking into the building. His pithy summation revealed a powerful underlying truth: an unwillingness to consider exceptional possibilities, to think beyond the accepted norm, had prevented building security and the police from securing the premises and solving the crime.

Bill took advantage of a psychological limitation that is so common it is almost invisible: routine thinking. So much of human behaviour and life in general is based on conventions, expected norms, and the parameters of what usually occurs. He repeatedly exploited this in aid of unethical goals, but his story prompts us to consider what might be possible if we overcome routine thinking in relation to ourselves.

You can be, do, and have more than you previously thought

IN MY YEARS practising as a psychologist, one of the most consistent observations I've made is how frequently people underestimate their capacity to change. They underestimate how much and how quickly it is possible to alter their life course, and what their potential would be if they acted persistently in aid of their goals. The human tendency to assume consistency means we assume that our future will reflect what's happened in the past. Just like the case of Bill Mason's heist, we are prone to failures of imagination. Opening up the possibility of an improved future requires imagination and audacity. We need to give ourselves permission to think beyond normal expectations to what extraordinary things might be possible.

In the Florida heist, everyone except Bill was a victim of routine thinking. They couldn't conceive of an ordinary-looking, older man simply walking in to the building to commit a major crime. Not only did Bill conceive of this plan, the fact that others could *not* made it easier for him to pull off an extraordinary misdeed. No matter what others think you can or can't do, what counts is what you can *imagine* yourself doing.

Your extraordinary future is a jewel waiting for you

Unlike Bill, we're not focused on taking something precious from somebody else. Our most devastating failures of imagination relate to not realising our most fulfilling, exhilarating, and meaningful life possible. When a normal, imperfect human being attains their best possible life, it is indeed something very rare and precious. Extraordinary outcomes start with thinking about extraordinary possibilities. They require us to break free from the routine of *what we've always done.*

Admittedly, claiming your best possible future does require a bit of jewel thief attitude: breaking the rules of expectation, daring to take risks, and a lingering sense that you're getting away with something. Now that your internal resources are full to the brim with wellbeing and you have a psychological skill set that puts you ahead of the pack, what's next? If you act like Bill Mason scoping out his next big haul, and imagine the extraordinary happening in your own life, what possibilities come to mind? Having a clear target on which to focus the scope of your intention is the final ingredient in the recipe of principles contained in this book.

You now have a formula for making your dreams a reality.

Your success formula

When you combine robust wellbeing and psychological know-how with a systematic approach to tackling difficult but meaningful things, and the audacity to imagine your extraordinary future, you have a recipe for extraordinary success. This formula clearly explains how we can transcend the typical habits of those around us, who either fail to proactively maintain their wellbeing, lack psychological skills, or are driven by passive forces and routine thinking. The most incredible realisation here is that *none of this requires a revolution in how you live your life.* Instead it requires a quiet, conscious diligence in applying what you've learned. Measured, consistent changes, informed by awareness of your best possible nature, take seeming insignificant differences between one action or another and transforms them into a vastly better outcome. A left turn here or a right turn there, a yes or a no, multiplied across a lifetime.

And here is the most powerful lesson available to us all: exceptional lives, rich with the rewards and joy of accomplishment, do not require grandiose affirmation and approval. More often the true exemplar is unassuming, determined, and humble. External accolades pale in comparison to the triumph of personal development: fulfilled potential. A best possible life, no matter the starting point. The contentment of a pioneer who has explored themselves and mastered their own journey. Conquerors masquerading as ordinary people. An incredible and rewarding adventure available to the likes of you and me.

ACKNOWLEDGEMENTS

Huge thanks to:

My wife Annabel for her love and support.

My Editor, Alida Winternheimer, for taking my very rough diamond of a manuscript and helping me turn it into a book I can be proud of.

Simon Wilksch, Anna Bouchard, and Corey Rushworth for believing in me.

Mum and Dad for teaching me to believe in myself.

Jane Cooper, Lisa Irvine, Mac Macpherson, David Scott, and all my mentors and friends from Flinders University.

Nick Lee, my co-Director at Healthy Minds Education & Training, for sharing my vision and helping make it a reality.

AUTHOR REQUEST

As an independent author-publisher, I am grateful to you, the reader, for having shown an interest in this book. If you have found it helpful, please help others find out about it by leaving a review on the platform from which you purchased it.

Thank you for your support.

Yours sincerely,

Tom Nehmy

☆ ☆ ☆ ☆ ☆

Printed in Great Britain
by Amazon

59501765R00136